The Official Slacker Handbook

Sarah Dunn

WARNER BOOKS

A Time Warner Company

D0019220

Warner Books, Inc.
1271 Avenue of the Americas
New York, NY 10020

 A Time Warner Company

Printed in the United States of America

First Printing: November 1994

10 9 8 7 6 5 4 3 2 1

Library of Congress Cataloging-in-Publication Data
Dunn, Sarah.
    The Official Slacker Handbook / Sarah Dunn.
    p.   cm.
    ISBN 0-446-67058-8
            I. Title.
PN6162.D85   1994
818'.5407--dc20   94-18662
                         CIP

Book design by Eli Har-dof
Cover design by Julia Kushnirsky
Cover illustration by Janet Woolley
Interior illustrations by
Dmitry Kushnirsky

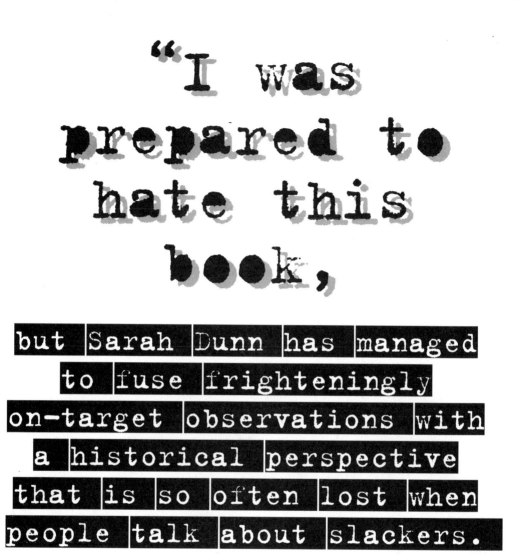

"I was prepared to hate this book, but Sarah Dunn has managed to fuse frighteningly on-target observations with a historical perspective that is so often lost when people talk about slackers. A tremendously funny book."

—Richard Linklater, director of *Slacker, Dazed and Confused,* and *Before Sunrise*

**For Nana,
who is not a slacker**

ACKNOWLEDGMENTS

I'd like to thank Nick Ellison, whose tireless efforts on my behalf have surpassed what could be expected of any mortal, and who has become both friend and agent. Also thanks to Mauro DiPreta, who not only superbly edited and shepherded this manuscript through production, but also demonstrated the sort of trust that only a slacker can appreciate when he gave me the Warner Books Federal Express account number.

David Warner, editor of the Philadelphia *City Paper*, can be held largely responsible for what has become of my career; I owe him a lot, not the least of which are about twenty columns that I was too lazy to write while working on this project. Thanks are also owed to Richard Linklater, who provided the inspiration for this book and an entire generation with his seminal film *Slacker*. Go rent it.

I, perhaps unwisely, elected to work with a few slackers in order to complete this book. I never got any of their work on time, but when I got it, it was great. Thanks to Christopher Borromeo, for his photos, Chris Gore, editor of *Film Threat* magazine, for the Slacker Film Round-up, and Katherine Dahlsgaard, for her herculean efforts as my research assistant. I also owe a huge debt to Bumby Vanover who was influential in both the conception and delivery of this book; at least half the chromosomes rightly belong to him.

Thanks to Alice Wood, for her enthusiasm and encouragement, and Michael Lynn-Hale, who did her best to keep me sane.

Countless people offered up their thoughts, theories, and occasionally even unsolicited intimate details about their personal lives in order to further my slack education, but I can say quite honestly that without hours of sitting in Makam's Kitchen drinking coffee with a few of them, this book would never have been written. My utmost gratitude goes to: Paul Dellevigne, Steven Eckstein, and Greg Swartzentruber. Also, special thanks to Howard Gensler, Devin Williams, Mick Hans, and Charlie Vanover.

Thanks to John Petrie, Rich Carter, Shawn Leahy, and Jan Schiffman of the as-yet-unsigned Philly-based band Trouser, and Tom Dolan, Joe DeBlasio, and Katherine of the as-yet-unsigned Philly-based band New Age Killers. Also thanks are due to Gina Bittner, Alex DuComb, Margit Detweiler, and Bruce Schimmel of the Philadelphia *City Paper*.

I'd like to express my appreciation for the following individuals, who let me pick their brains, steal their ideas, and/or take their pictures: Lee Wybranski, Lori Marks, Michael Geszel, Alexander Jay Storman, Solomon Wise, Thomas Cannon, Ruth Schwechtje, David J. Brown, Dunkin, Camille Becerra, Edouard Bance, Lisa Krieger, Ananda White, Katherine

Dahlsgaard, Kelly McQuain, Patrick Kelly, Hawk, Sebastian Havoc Oz, Lorne Peart, Joe Jensen, Andrew J. Turner, Kevin L. Burrows, John Cannon, Peter Wilson, Heather Moyer, cph, James Andrews, Ryan Litts, Noel Ellerbe, Autumn Russo, Dominic Marano, Frank Iaquinta, Aaron Ferranti, Christopher Miller, Jim Smith, Jeff Howard, John DelHousaye, Tyler McGrath, Adam Bogage, Jacqueline Walter, Casper, Dana Wachs, Anastasia Goldman, Kathryn M. Sibrel, Debi Paoli, Paul Compano, Leslie Brauman, Raegan Fogg, Oddessa, Cory Sprenkle, Darin Basile, Timothy J. Kline, Terry L. Wade, James Eagle, Jacob Lavin, Kelly McBride, Jason McKibben, Eric Crittenden, Elisabeth Hammer, Melissa Ferus, Dana Witengier, Mpozi Tolbert, Juliana Shinn, Moses Johnson, Salvator Anthony Cinqu, Howard Martin, Jacob Lavin, Ned Sonstein, Anna Thea Conrad, Jesse Hershey, Adam Schuler, Shabut Hameed, Raul Wiznitzer, Ted Cohen, and Johnathon Goldstein.

For help with conspiracy theories I turned to a handful of nameless anti-social loners in various cafes as well as to *Conspiracies, Cover-Ups and Crimes*, by Jonathan Vankin, The *Illuminatus Trilogy*, by Robert Shea and Robert Anton Wilson, and *The UFO Guidebook*, by Norman J. Briazack and Simon Mennick.

Thanks to the board and benefactors of Ledig House, who were kind enough to provide me with free food and shelter for two months so I could live in true slack fashion while finishing up my manuscript. Thanks to Elaine Smollin and Helmut Frielinghaus for their encouragement and support. Also thanks to the members of Sword & Spoon, past and present, who helped me shape my own *weltanschauung*.

Thanks for all of their love and help to: Nancy, Susanne, Jean, John, Owen, Mark, Linda, Horace, Amy, Stephanie, Barbara, Shiloah, and Joy.

Thanks to my parents—Pete Dunn and Joe and Carolyn Davis—encouraging me, praying for me, and floating me the occasional loan (which, if this book goes platinum, I just might pay back). Also thanks to Aunt Sue, Grandma Dunn, Jeff, Kati, and Webb.

Finally, thanks to David Urso, who, more than anyone else, supported and encouraged me while writing this book. Winnona Forever.

CONTENTS

HOPPING INTO THE SLACK

intro duction

It is the inalienable right of every man, woman, and child to work as little as humanly possible. Looking, acting, and ultimately being slack is no longer restricted to an elite minority of twenty-four-year-olds lucky enough to spend their days drinking coffee in smoke-filled cafes and writing delicate poems littered with obscenities. You don't even have to have read Bukowski. In this decade of shame and self-loathing anyone can be a cynical destitute genius. It's only fair.

The Official Slacker Handbook will help you in your transformation from gainfully-employed sane person to poverty-stricken malcontent. For slacking is much more than just battling adult-onset acne and sleeping til noon—it's making your way through a hermetic subculture in which important subtleties abound. Within this book lies the sort of information that would make even the most intrepid zeitgeist-forging slacker gape: where to live, what to wear, what to read, what to tell people you've read, how to steal things from work, how to forestall utility termination — even how to make hallucinogenic drugs from basic household chemicals. It includes advice on choosing day jobs, house pets, live-in lovers, tattoo designs, and conspiracy theories. It covers everything from cafe etiquette to sex etiquette, from serial killers to suicidal artists, from hooking up to breaking up.

So stop thinking you're a lost cause just because you own a couch that's never been propped against a curb on trash day. Even the most die-hard slacker had to learn to struggle with timeless existential questions and cultivate his deathlike pallor. Remember: Slackers don't have to be overeducated Caucasian males who were raised in the suburbs in the Seventies and are deluded about their creative abilities. But they do have to read this book. Even if they do it standing up in the corner of the bookstore. It's the ultimate shortcut. It's alpha prime.

Slack Like Me

SLACKING THROUGHOUT

THROUGHOUT

Somerset, England, 1797

Education history: Cambridge dropout
Drug of choice: Opium
Formative experience: The French Revolution
Signature affectation: Rumpled ascot
Night table reading: Immanuel Kant's *Groundwork of the Metaphysic of Ethics*
***Weltanschauung*-shaking assassination:** Marie Antoinette
Sexual mores broken: Fell unhappily in love with prudish sister-in-law
Basic philosophical conflict: Man vs. Nature
Hallmark of creative efforts: Shocking subject matter presented in simple, unpoetic style with thinly disguised autobiographical content
Day job: Disgruntled landbearing aristocrat

Paris, 1922

Education history: Princeton dropout
Drug of choice: Jug wine
Formative experience: Discovery that he could invite women back to his studio and make them disrobe nearly convinced him to give up fiction and dedicate his life to painting
Signature affectation: Beat-up walking stick and pipe
Night table reading: James Joyce's *Ulysses*
***Weltanschauung*-shaking assassination:** Archduke Ferdinand
Sexual mores broken: Associated with known homosexuals
Basic philosophical conflict: Man vs. Man
Hallmark of creative efforts: Shocking subject matter presented in simple, unpoetic style with thinly disguised autobiographical content
Day job: Disgruntled dairy fortune heir

HISTORY

San Francisco, 1967

Education history: High school dropout

Drug of choice: Ditch weed

Formative experience: Hallucinogen-induced late-night vision of Alexander Pope convinced him to dedicate his life to poetry

Signature affectation: Black turtle-neck

Night table reading: Charles Bukowski's *The Post Office*

***Weltanschauung*-shaking assassination:** John F. Kennedy

Sexual mores broken: Opted to have sex with his brother-in-law

Basic philosophical conflict: Man vs. Society

Hallmark of creative efforts: Shocking subject matter presented in simple, unpoetic style with thinly disguised autobiographical content

Day job: Disgruntled trust-fund drifter

austin, 1994

Education history: Film school dropout

Drug of choice: Unfiltered Camels and black coffee

Formative experience: Discovery that Heinz ketchup's "57 varieties" was secret Illuminati codescript (right along with the pyramid with the eye on the back of the dollar bill) convinced him to resign himself to political and economic apathy

Signature affectation: Knit cap

Night table reading: Robert Graysmith's *Who Killed Bob Crane?*

***Weltanschauung*-shaking assassination:** Ronald Reagan (attempted)

Sexual mores broken: Stuns dominant culture by frequently being too lazy to have sex

Basic philosophical conflict: Man vs. Me

Hallmark of creative efforts: Shocking subject matter presented in simple, unpoetic style with thinly disguised autobiographical content

Day job: Disgruntled coat check boy

THE SLACK SENSIBILITY

THE SLACK SENSIBILITY IS PART OLD-FASHIONED BOHEMIANISM AND PART FIN DE SIÈCLE EXHAUSTION, PLACED AGAINST THE BACKDROP OF A CRAPPY RECESSION AND INTOLERABLE SUBURBAN IRONY. IN SOME IT BLOSSOMS INTO A HAPPY-GO-LUCKY PROLONGED ADOLESCENCE IN WHICH THE SATISFACTION THAT COMES FROM TRASH-PICKING *BJ AND THE BEAR* LUNCHBOXES AND MAKING UP SONGS CALLED "JEWISH HOAGIE" TAKES THE PLACE OF SCALING THE CORPORATE LADDER AND SPAWNING KIDS. OTHERS ELECT TO PICK AT THE SCABS OF THEIR PSYCHE AND QUICKLY DEGENERATE INTO A MOUND OF BROODING APATHY AND DESPAIR. EITHER WAY, THEY SHARE A FEW IDEALS THAT TRANSCEND MERE FASHION OR MUSIC, A COMMON SENSIBILITY THAT ALSO HAPPENS TO BE, AS ASTUTE CULTURAL COMMENTATORS WILL SURELY NOTE, NOTHING NEW:

CONSCIOUS NON-PARTICIPATION

Metaphysical paralysis? TV-induced inertia? Plain old-fashioned laziness? A lot has been said about the slacker's trademark indolence, but the point must be made that deliberately opting out of socially-recognized forms of activity isn't the same thing as stumbling into inaction. If you refuse to be a cog in our economic machine you become, *de facto*, a detached spectator with a lot of free time on your hands.

REJECTION OF CONSUMERISM

This isn't to say that slackers have rejected *materialism*. They don't aspire to give away their CD collections and live like Gandhi. Quite the contrary. But, put plainly, rejecting the nose-to-the-grindstone lifestyle that's founded upon the ethic of Purchasing New Things isn't the same as rejecting the ethic of Mooching, Shoplifting, and Stealing them.

CONTEMPT FOR CORPORATE AMERICA

THE NUMBER OF FETID CORPSES AND DISMEMBERED KITTENS THAT CAN BE LEFT AT THE DOORSTEP OF CORPORATE AMERICA DEFIES CALCULATION. VAGUE SLACK ANTI-ESTABLISHMENT LEANINGS FIND THEIR IDEAL TARGET IN THIS EVIL FACELESS BEHEMOTH. CHEMICAL CORPORATIONS THAT TOXIFY THE WATER TABLE? PHARMACEUTICAL COMPANIES THAT STICK IT TO AIDS SURVIVORS? THE GAP, WHO APPROPRIATED SLACK FLANNEL SHIRTS AND THEN SOLD THEM IN SUBURBAN SHOPPING MALLS FOR FORTY-FOUR BUCKS? ALAS, NO ONE IS IMMUNE.

CULTIVA-TION OF THE INNER Landscape

Even if at times he has little else, the slacker has a lively inner world. In its highest form, slacking is not unlike coasting through in a non-degree post-bac program of your own devising. Either way, the locus of activity takes place between the ears, for some in the highly developed cerebral cortex, for others in the more humble brain stem and cerebellum.

REFUSAL TO BE CATE-GORIZED

The slacker hates to be categorized. In fact, he will go so far as to claim that he is *impossible* to categorize. Suggest to him that his chronic malaise and vague dissatisfaction with life is nothing more than part of a widespread generational impulse and you'll quickly

be shown the door. Needless to say, slackers are amazingly quick to lob flaming insults at anyone who dares to claim to speak about them, to them or — God forbid — *for* them.

UNTAPPED RAGE

SLACKERS DON'T WANT TO BE CATEGORIZED, LARGELY BECAUSE THEY'VE SPENT THEIR LIVES WITNESSING THE BABY BOOMERS' UNDYING LOVE FOR THE CONCEPT OF GROUP IDENTITY AND THE UNDISGUISED GLEE THEY EXHIBIT WHEN ONE OF THEIR CONTEM-PORARIES TRIES TO PIGEONHOLE THEM WITH A NEW DEFINING CHARACTERISTIC. THE BOOMERS LOVE TO INVENT MAGAZINES ABOUT THEMSELVES, MAGAZINES THAT TELL THEM HOW IMPORTANT AND NOBLE AND GOOD THEY ARE, MAGAZINES THAT ASSURE THEM THAT IT'S COOL TO BE CROTCHETY AND POST-MENOPAUSAL AND IMPOTENT, AND MAGA-ZINES THAT—THIRTY YEARS FROM NOW—WILL CONVINCE THEM THAT IT'S HIP TO BE DEAD. (SLACKERS, QUITE UNDERSTANDABLY, LOOK ON IN HORROR.)

The Slack Pantheon

The Lotus Eaters —9th century B.C.

A WHOLE TRIBE OF SLACKERS FEATURED IN HOMER'S EPIC POEM *THE ODYSSEY*. LIVED ON AN ISLAND OFF THE NORTH AFRICAN COAST AND ATE ONLY FROM THE LOTUS TREE, THE EFFECT OF WHICH WAS TO MAKE THEM WASTOIDS AND LAYABOUTS (SORT OF LIKE KOALAS AND THEIR EUCALYPTUS LEAVES). HAVE COME TO SYMBOLIZE LIVING IN EASE AND LUXURY. ODYSSEUS AND HIS FELLOW SAILORS ENCOUNTERED THEM IN THE NINTH BOOK OF *THE ODYSSEY*: "I SENT AWAY SOME OF MY COMRADES TO FIND WHAT MANNER OF HUMAN BEINGS WERE THOSE WHO LIVED HERE. THEY WENT AT ONCE AND SOON WERE AMONG THE LOTUS EATERS, WHO HAD NO THOUGHTS OF MAKING AWAY WITH MY COMPANIONS, BUT GAVE THEM LOTUS TO TASTE INSTEAD. THOSE OF MY MEN WHO ATE THE HONEY-SWEET LOTUS FRUIT HAD NO DESIRE TO RETRACE THEIR STEPS AND COME BACK WITH NEWS: THEIR ONLY WISH WAS TO LINGER THERE WITH THE LOTUS EATERS, TO FEED ON THE FRUIT AND PUT ASIDE ALL THOUGHT OF A VOYAGE HOME. THESE MEN I THEN FORCED BACK TO THE SHIPS; THEY WERE SHEDDING TEARS BUT I MADE THEM GO."

Siddhartha Gautama 563-483 B.C. (approx.)

Also known as Buddha, or "the enlightened one." Born a prince and raised in luxury. AT AGE OF TWENTY-NINE DID THAT DOWNWARDLY MOBILE THING AND FORSOOK ALL HIS FINERIES TO WANDER AROUND AND FIND THE END TO THE INNATE CONDITION OF HUMAN SUFFERING. Sat under a tree for quite some time and yet still managed to reach enlightenment (sort of, and yet not, like Newton). **Hung out with the guys** for the next forty-five years, living off the donations of wealthy lay devotees. His third Noble Truth, that suffering has a cessation, was the inspiration

for the name of the band that fathered all ye holy grunge (Nirvana).

Diogenes
412-323 B.C. (approx.)

Greek Cynic philosopher. Believed in the simple life; hence, lived in a barrel. Dispensed with his only kitchen utensil, a cup (probably a coffee mug), when he saw some impoverished peasant drink with his hands. Really into tanning, apparently, because when Alexander the Great asked what he could do for him, Diogenes answered, *"Only step out of my sunlight." Had (surprise) great contempt for his own generation and wandered around with a lit lantern in broad daylight looking for an honest man (ha!).

Socrates
469-399 B.C. (approx.)

GREEK PHILOSOPHER. NEGLECTED HIS OWN AFFAIRS. DIDN'T EVEN BOTHER TO GO INTO PUBLIC SERVICE (AN EXPECTED THING BACK IN THOSE DAYS IN ATHENS). WANDERED AROUND FOR THE MAJORITY OF HIS LIFE AVOIDING HIS WIFE AND HANGING OUT WITH THE GUYS DISCUSSING VIRTUE, JUSTICE, AND ETHICS WHEREVER FELLOW CITIZENS CONGREGATED. LIKED TO WAX PHILOSOPHIC ABOUT HOW HE SHOULD RUN THE CITY, I.E., HE CONSTANTLY FANTASIZED ABOUT A CITY WHERE PHILOSOPHERS (WORTHLESS LAYABOUTS) WOULD BE KINGS (SORT OF LIKE THE TYPICAL FANTASY ALL TWENTIETH CENTURY SLACKERS HAVE OF STARRING IN THEIR OWN NETWORK LATE-NIGHT TV TALK SHOW).

Conon and His Triballi
370s B.C.

Essentially a band of well-to-do young street toughs in Athens. Took their name from a tribe of brigand Thracian people (Thrace is now pretty much Turkey) who ravaged the coast in 376. Rich and having nothing better to do, they went on drinking rampages, crashed parties, committed unspecified acts of hooliganism, and stole the sacrificed pigs (these were sacrificed to Hecate at the beginning of every month) off of people's doorsteps to eat like the poor people did, only they weren't poor, just spoiled brats, blatantly thumbing their noses at established religion. Immortalized in one of Demosthenes' private orations (he is the most famous classical orator —he basically wrote speeches for people to give in court, sort of like a lawyer) where a proper young man named Ariston brought Conon and his son to court for allegedly unprovokedly attacking him and his slaves in a drunken brawl and stealing his cape, etc. Conon tried to pass it off as just harmless Triballi antics; polite society in Athens saw these kids merely as unruly idlers and wastrels.

HAMLET, PRINCE OF DENMARK
B. 1601 (APPROX.)

Prince of Indecision. Perpetually miserable, a layabout, still living at home even at the age of thirty-five. Given to philosophical rhapsodies on the nature of humanity rather than actually getting anything accomplished (like killing his stepdad).

Too lazy to go out and get himself a real girlfriend, he kept it in the family. Hung out with colorful folk such as wandering actors and grave diggers. Suicidal.

Jesus
4 B.C.-30 A.D.

ALSO KNOWN AS "THE MESSIAH" OR "CHRIST." THE MOST AGGRESSIVELY DOWNWARDLY MOBILE OF THE BUNCH, AS HE WAS, AFTER ALL, THE SON OF GOD. BASICALLY, HIS REAL FATHER WAS CEO OF THE WORLD, AND JESUS SETTLED FOR THE LIFE OF AN ITINERANT PREACHER. HIS STEPDAD, JOSEPH, HAD A JOB AS A CARPENTER IN HIS COMPANY ALL LINED UP FOR JESUS, BUT HE DECLINED AND INSTEAD CHOSE A LIFE OF **HANGING OUT WITH THE GUYS.** HE HAD COOL ACQUAINTANCES LIKE PROSTITUTES AND ASYLUM ESCAPEES. PEOPLE HUNG OUT WITH HIM BECAUSE HE HAD CHARISMA.

Samuel T. Coleridge
1172-1834

English poet and arguably the most influential figure of the English Romantic Movement. Notorious for never finishing anything and having failed literary pursuits. Authored the aborted *Kubla Kahn* and *Ode to Dejection*. A precocious and dreamy child; he said of himself, "I became very vain, and despised most of the boys that were at all near my own age, and before I was eight years old I was a character. Sensibility, imagination, vanity, sloth, and feelings of deep and bitter contempt for all who traversed the orbit of my understanding, were even then prominent and manifest."

Dropped out of Jesus College, Cambridge, in 1793, then was forced to return by his family; however, in 1794 he was kicked out for hanging out with Robert Southey, a young radical. Had several big schemes that never came to fruition, among them to establish a pantioscratic community in Pennsylvania, and publication of a literary magazine, *Watchman*, which failed after ten issues, as did another publication, *Friend*. Much of his work, such as *Opus Maximum*, was left unfinished. Opium addict and (allegedly) quite a plagiarizer.

Gioacchino Rossini
1792-1868

Italian composer. Also a notorious self-plagiarizer, Rossini had a habit of using arias from his former operas in his new ones. Hence, his most famous opera, The *Barber of Seville*, was written in thirteen days.

Rossini himself wrote about his method of work: "WAIT UNTIL THE EVENING BEFORE THE OPENING NIGHT. NOTHING PRIMES INSPIRATION MORE THAN NECESSITY, WHETHER IT BE THE PRESENCE OF A COPYIST WAITING FOR YOUR WORK, OR THE PRODDING OF AN IMPRESARIO TEARING HIS HAIR. . . . I WROTE THE OVERTURE TO *LA GAZZA* THE DAY OF ITS OPENING IN THE THEATER ITSELF, WHERE I WAS IMPRISONED BY THE DIRECTOR AND UNDER THE SURVEILLANCE OF THE STAGEHANDS WHO WERE INSTRUCTED TO THROW MY ORIGINAL TEXT THROUGH THE WINDOW, PAGE BY PAGE, TO THE COPYISTS WAITING BELOW TO TRANSCRIBE IT." He was charismatic, had wit and sparkle, and was very gifted. Said, "Bring me the laundry list and I will set it to music." Got really fat and rich. Stopped composing in 1829 and didn't write another note for publication (that's for thirty-nine *years*).

Rip Van Winkle
1819

Hero of a folktale by Washington Irving. Rip and his dog, Wolf, escape his nagging wife by heading up to the Catskills before the Revolutionary War. He meets a bunch of dwarfs, with whom he proceeds to bowl and get drunk. Rip passes out like a frat boy. He wakes up twenty years later and his wife is dead. So it worked.

Bartleby the Scrivener
1853

Hero of the short story by Herman Melville. The narrator of the story runs a law firm on Wall Street and hires Bartleby to copy and proofread legal documents (like a pre-slack paralegal). Soon enough Bartleby will only stare at a wall and answers all requests for work with the statement "I would prefer not to." The narrator can't get Bartleby to even leave the office, much less to work, so he moves. Bartleby dies of starvation.

Oblomov
1859

HERO OF THE SAME-NAMED NOVEL BY IVAN GONCHAROV. ILYA ILYICH OBLOMOV IS AN UTTERLY INACTIVE RUSSIAN LANDOWNER IN ST. PETERSBURG. HE IS THE EMBODIMENT OF PHYSICAL AND MENTAL LAZINESS, LIES ON HIS COUCH ALL DAY, ONLY WEARS HIS ROBE AND SLIPPERS, AND INDULGES IN REVERIES AND QUARRELS WITH HIS SERVANT. HE DIES IN FINANCIAL RUIN BECAUSE HE WON'T GET OFF THE COUCH TO MANAGE HIS ESTATE.

Franz Kafka
1883-1924

PRAGUE AUTHOR. PUBLISHED BARELY ANYTHING, PRESUMABLY BECAUSE HE WAS TOO BUSY WRITING IN HIS JOURNALS OR TO HIS FRIENDS. MOST OF HIS STUFF WAS LEFT UNFINISHED. DIDN'T MOVE OUT OF HIS PARENTS' HOUSE UNTIL HE WAS THIRTY-FIVE. KEPT GETTING ENGAGED AND BREAKING IT OFF. SUICIDAL. WORKED AS A CLERK IN AN INSURANCE AGENCY FROM 8 A.M. TO 3 P.M. WITH NO BREAK SO HE COULD FREE UP HIS TIME FOR WRITING. MOST OF WHICH HE NEVER PUBLISHED.

Marcel Duchamp
1887-1968

French-American painter. Produced a small body of work, mostly before 1925, when he retired to play chess. Began by painting—among his works were the notorious *Sex* *Machine* series —then did the Ready-Made thing, such as *Bicycle Wheel* and *Fountain* (a urinal). Drew a mustache on the Mona Lisa. One of the founders of Dada.

slackers don't jog

JIM FIXX'S UNTIMELY DEATH IN 1984 IS LODGED IN THE SLACK BRAIN, JUST TO THE LEFT OF JOHN BELUSHI'S OVERDOSE AND DIRECTLY BENEATH THE LATE-BREAKING DETAILS OF BOB CRANE'S GRISLY S&M SLAYING. JIM FIXX'S DEATH WAS THE BEGINNING OF THE END FOR A GENERATION THAT WOULD GO ON TO MAKE A HABIT OF LOSING ITS INNOCENCE, AND PROOF POSITIVE THAT MOST OF WHAT YOU WERE TOLD WHILE GROWING UP IN THE '70S WERE NOTHING BUT BOLDFACE LIES.

Here's a smattering of what you've learned since:

Air: bad
Tap water: toxic
Sunshine: carcinogenic
Sex: lethal
College degree: worthless
The Four Food Groups: Unsound self-promotional fiction manufactured by powerful meat and dairy lobbies
The zoo: animal prison
Jody and Buffy: drug addicts
Daisy Duke: infamous short-shorts butt shots actually the handiwork of stunt woman stand-in
The Brady Household: scene of twisted Oedipal liaison
Dr. Doolittle: culturally insensitive racist imperialist
The Jackson Five: cadre of freaks terrorized by abusive father and enabling mother
Barbie: nipple-less, de-sexed root of teenage eating disorders, materialism, and countless sexual hang-ups

Maynard G. Krebs 1959

Slack sidekick to Dobie Gillis on the popular TV show *The Many Loves of Dobie Gillis*, played by Bob Denver. His most oft-remarked remark was the exclamation *"Work??!!"* whenever anyone suggested that he get a job. Was nearly written out of the show after the first few episodes, and was represented by Dobie when court-martialed for refusing to shave off his trademark goatee.

A Day in the Life of a Slacker

10:52 A.M.: Glorious sleep

10:53 A.M.: Awaken when you are disturbed by the wheezy breathing of your housemate as he shuffles around in the hallway outside your bedroom.

10:57 A.M.: Fall back to sleep.

11:34 A.M.: Wake up again. Elect to lay in bed awhile longer so you can stare at the ceiling and think.

12:45 P.M.: Plan the world tour you would take if any of your relatives happened to die and handed you a pile of money.

1:33 P.M.: Sit down with a cup of coffee and read the new paper.

1:48 P.M.: Realize that you write much better than any of the nationally syndicated editorial columnists that appear in your local paper. Wonder how much money they make.

1:52 P.M.: Peruse an op-ed article stating that your generation represents "the final exhaustion of civilization." Resolve to fire off a scathing yet piquant rebuttal.

2:00 P.M.: Watch Hogan's Heroes.

2:30 P.M.: Watch second installment of Hogan's Heroes.

2:42 P.M.: Commercial break. Decide to go to work on your newest major project —a flow chart in which you are attempting to categorize and classify every philosopher throughout time according to your very own top secret rating system —just as soon as you find out how this episode ends.

3:14 P.M.: Leave the house and wander around aimlessly.

3:45 P.M.: Find yourself at a cafe. Get a cup of coffee and set to work on The Chart.

3:48 P.M.: Get momentarily stumped by Schopenhauer. Skip him for the time being and forge ahead to Herbert Spencer.

4:30 P.M.: Show your groundbreaking flowchart to a fellow cafe-goer. Attempt to impress upon him the sheer magnitude of the task you have set yourself.

4:31 P.M.: Shrink back in horror when he blows smoke in your face and says, "Dude, it's just a list of names."

4:35 P.M.: Figure maybe you would like to work with your hands. To learn how to make something.

4:37 P.M.: Realize you will be in direct competition with thousands of fleet-fingered peasants from Bangladesh. Your only career options seem to be fifteen minutes of fame or years of manning the

	frothing machine at Orange Julius.
5:20 P.M.:	Return home.
5:27 P.M.:	Take a nap.
7:32 P.M.:	Get out of bed. "Borrow" a box of your house-mate's Kraft Macaroni and Cheese for dinner.
7:56 P.M.:	Resolve to build your own log cabin out in the woods and live off the fat of the land. Begin drawing up some preliminary floor plans inside your crisp new notebook.
8:48 P.M.:	Hunker down with Schopenhauer.
9:05 P.M.:	Partake in shouting match with your housemate over the mysterious disappearance of a box of Kraft Macaroni and Cheese.
9:33 P.M.:	Storm out of the house, saying, "Geez, man, I'm not sure I can live with this sort of distrust. Not in my own home."
9:45 P.M.:	Elect to embark on a drinking binge.
9:46 P.M.:	Root through your pockets. Come up with seventy three cents and a prodigious clump of lint.
9:48 P.M.:	Take a long, reflective walk.
10:13 P.M.:	Decide that life's increasing randomness does not let you believe the lies that could make you more normal. Wish you had a pencil so you could write this down.
11:05 P.M.:	Return home.
11:15 P.M.:	Actively ignore the rumblings of your housemate.
11:30 P.M.:	Putter around your room.
11:48 P.M.:	Rake the sand in your Zen rock garden.
12:15 A.M.:	Alphabetize your cassettes.
12:33 A.M.:	Practice your dart game.
1:00 A.M.:	Assume the fetal position for late night infomercial viewing.
1:26 A.M.:	Stare near-crippling bout of existential angst in the face.
1:57 A.M.:	Once again, glorious sleep.

Mastering Sleep

If there is one common bond, one shared experience that draws slackers together, it is one that takes place between the sheets—shades pulled down against the blazing sun, housemates plodding noisily down the hall, jackhammers pounding the asphalt outside—alone. The connoisseurship of sleep is the essence of slack. Cheaper than a forty, more soothing than a twelve-hour *Family Affair* marathon on cable, unlikely to cause vital clumps of neurons to misfire in later life, sleep transcends mere biological imperative and quickly becomes a way of life. As the first line of attack against the tyranny of reality, a three-hour-long nap rarely fails.

If you find sleep to be anything less than a pleasure bordering on the sublime, the life of a slacker is probably not for you. For sleep—hours of it stretching into days, days into months —is slack's most tangible perk. And it's the perk of a career whose perks, quite often, are few and far between.

(Relaxed contemplation, not to be confused with sleep, consists of thinking while in a horizontal position. Ideally this takes place on the couch, in the afternoon, sometime after *Chico and the Man*. For the artist, the line between meaningful contemplation and actual creation is so fine that it is, for all intents and purposes, nonexistent. Thus an afternoon of lounging on the couch, eyelids at half-mast, acid-free notepad splayed open on one's chest, is easily as good as a few hours of sketching old people while sitting on a park bench.)

ARE YOU A SLACKER?
Quiz #1

Instructions: Choose the answer that *best* matches your own:

1. Before exiting the employee restroom at work you instinctively:
   - a) Wash your hands thoroughly
   - b) Check your gums for signs of receding
   - c) Steal several rolls of toilet paper

2. You know a relationship is on the rocks when:
   - a) You haven't gone out to dinner in six months
   - b) You haven't had sex in six months
   - c) One of you gets a real job

3. Your aesthetic philosophy could best be summed up with the phrase:
   - a) "Subvert the dominant paradigm"
   - b) "Live the question"
   - c) "Novels are hard but poetry's easy"

4. Your relationship with your parents would run much smoother if only they would:
   - a) Quit pestering you about applying to law school
   - b) Stop frittering away your inheritance on Carnival Cruises
   - c) Install a cash machine on the front lawn

5. A visitor to your home would be able to find:
   - a) Coffee filters in the kitchen, socks in the bed, and dirty dishes on the toilet tank
   - b) Dirty dishes in the kitchen, coffee filters in the bed, and socks on the toilet tank
   - c) Socks in the kitchen, dirty dishes in the bed, and coffee filters on the toilet tank

The slack answer, in each case, is "c."

SLACKING THROUGH ACADEMIA

COLLEGE:

COLLEGE:

THE FOUR-YEAR PLAN:

DESIGNED FOR PEOPLE WHO LACK BOTH IMAGINATION AND PANACHE, THE FOUR-YEAR PLAN REQUIRES THAT YOU STICK WITH THE MAJOR YOUR FOLKS PICK OUT FOR YOU ON PARENTS' WEEKEND, PASS ALL YOUR EXAMS, AND TURN IN YOUR FINAL PAPERS MORE OR LESS ON TIME. DISTINCTLY UN-SLACK.

THE FIVE-YEAR PLAN:

A YEAR OF BREATHING ROOM CAN ALLOW FOR A CHANGE OF MAJOR, A CHANGE OF ACADEM-IC VENUE, A MINOR NERVOUS BREAKDOWN, A SMATTERING OF ABORTED CLASSES, OR A YEAR OF WANDERING AROUND THE COUNTRY IN AN ILL-FATED ATTEMPT TO FIND YOURSELF. UNFORTUNATELY, IT'S NOT ENOUGH TIME FOR ALL OF THE ABOVE.

THE SEVEN-YEAR PLAN:

GIVES YOU AMPLE TIME TO GO WORK ON AN OIL RIG, DESIGN YOUR OWN MULTIDEPARTMENTAL INTERDISCIPLINARY MAJOR, READ ALL OF DANTE IN THE ORIGINAL ITALIAN, BEGIN SEV-ERAL SHORT 16MM FILMS, AND COMPETE IN THE IDITAROD. ADDED BONUS: YOU CAN CON-TINUE TO DATE FRESHMEN WELL INTO YOUR THIRD DECADE.

THE ABSENCE OF A PLAN:

DESIGNED FOR INDIVIDUALS WHO WANT TO SPEND A DECADE TENDING BAR WHILE BEING DRIVEN QUIETLY INSANE BY A SLOUGH OF TWELVE-YEAR-OLD INCOMPLETES. IDEAL IF YOU CAN'T FIND AN ADVISOR WILL-ING TO SIGN OFF ON YOUR THESIS CONCEPT: "SEXUALITY, SEMIOTICS, AND *'STARSKY AND HUTCH.'*"

CHOOSING A MAJOR

UNFORTUNATELY, EVEN THE MOST PROGRESSIVE OF UNIVER-SITIES WILL BE RELUCTANT TO LET YOU MAJOR IN BROODING INTROSPECTION AND MINOR IN CAFFEINE STUDIES. THERE ARE A HANDFUL OF MAJORS, HOW-EVER, THAT WILL SEND YOU HURTLING DOWN THE SLACKING CAREER TRACK FASTER THAN YOU CAN SAY "BLUE BOOK EXAM." HERE ARE THE TOP TEN:

1. English
2. Film
3. Philosophy
4. Linguistics
5. Classical Studies
6. German
7. Theater
8. Creative writing
9. Intellectual history
10. Folklore

PACE YOURSELF

KNOW

For the collegiate slacker, knowing when to leave the shelter of academia is often the hardest thing of all. Some slackers never forge out on their own. They eventually graduate (at some point, it's hard not to), but then they go on to accumulate useless Master's degree after useless Master's degree, hoping with each one that it will result in a lucrative, meaningful, and easy new job. Finally they head for the Ph.D., never, of course, able to complete their dissertations, eventually descending into a bitter pit of self-loathing that they climb out of, periodically, so they can drink coffee in cafes with girls half their age.

Which is not necessarily a bad fate. There's no denying that staying in school has its advantages—the student loan people don't pester you to death, your parents still send you money—but at some point it's best to get on with your life and begin slacking full-time. You'll know you're ready to move on if you:

-smoke so much during finals that you occasionally hack up blood

-hate college radio and classic rock

-took every film class offered in the course catalog—even those that are only offered once a decade, when the school is able to attract just the right dissident filmmaker hailing from the appropriate former Soviet satellite—and then came to the realization one fine spring morning that all that film theory was a waste of your time and what you really should be doing is *making* movies.

-managed to get your wisdom teeth removed, your appendix taken out, your skin problem cleared up, and dozens of visits to expensive mental health care professionals, all paid for by your student health plan

-know how to construct a bong out of virtually any three common household items

-limit your social circle to a bunch of dropouts who live in a run-down house four blocks from campus

-notice your parents have stopped sending you money

I HATE MY JOB: SLACKING AT WORK

ADVENTURES IN SERFDOM:
Choosing a Day Job

> "Work, for me, is just being in a particular place for an extended period of time and not being allowed to leave."
> —Devin, a slacker

THE **REAL JOB** REQUIRES YOU TO WAKE UP EACH MORNING AT A PREDETERMINED HOUR, OFTEN ONE THAT COULD BEST BE DESCRIBED AS "UNGODLY." IT CALLS FOR A SUSTAINED EFFORT OVER A LENGTHY STRETCH OF HOURS—CUTTING INTO PRIME AFTERNOON TV VIEWING TIME, DRAMATICALLY REDUCING POTENTIAL NAPPING HOURS—AND LIMITS THE NUMBER OF VACATION DAYS YOU ARE ALLOWED IN A GIVEN YEAR WITHOUT EVEN TAKING INTO CONSIDERATION YOUR PLANS FOR A MOUNTAIN CLIMBING TRIP TO BOLIVIA. PERHAPS NEEDLESS TO SAY, THE REAL JOB IS ANATHEMA TO THE SLACKER.

The **Day Job**, on the other hand, is only tenuously tied to the concept of work if you define work as Webster does—"activity in which one exerts strength or faculties to do or perform something." Oddly enough, it often has nothing to do with the day either. A good Day Job is a job in which you are compensated for showing up periodically. Any requirements beyond that must be negotiated on a case-by-case basis.

So, sure you'll sit in the coat-check room and read. You might even partake of some free food and drink. Bum smokes from the bartender. Craft the occasional delicate poem littered with obscenities. But fold cloth napkins into elaborate origami peacocks? Increase your rate of coat-retrieval speed when a horde of angry people materializes outside your booth? Remember whose compact black umbrella is whose? What are you, nuts? When they start paying you for brain surgery, you'll start performing it.

The Day Jobs:

Bartender.
The indisputable pinnacle of achievement among food service industry employees: a most coveted slack job.

Bar back.
aka Aspiring bartender who refuses to wait tables. Marked by hours of schlepping kegs up and down stairs while trying to procure free shots from surly bar-tending slavelords.

Bellhop.
The chin-scraping obsequiousness and sycophantry that must be directed toward tiresome rich people makes this an especially easy job to lose.

Bicycle courier.
Must be able to weave through rush-hour traffic on a stolen mountain bike while under the influence of hallucinogenic drugs.

Bike store guy.
Learn how to do something with your hands, for once in your life. Expose yourself to the aesthetics of W-D40. Get intimate with a wrench.

Bookstore clerk.
Entry level position for aspiring First Novelists.

Cabbie.
Stash a can of Lysol in the glove compartment, stick a few urbane cartoons on the sliding plastic window, then pretend you can't speak English.

Cafe counterperson.
Such a coveted slack job in some cities that at least one young woman was turned down

8 Jobs YOU CAN DO While Wearing Your Pajamas:

there are two kinds of jobs in this world: those you can do in your pajamas and those you can't.

Here are eight you can:

1. DIAL-A-PSYCHIC
2. Freelance envelope licker
3. "Earn hundreds of dollars $$$ reading books in your home!"
4. Miracle Thigh Cream peddler
5. HUD refund processor
6. "Earn hundreds of dollars $$$ assembling products in your home!"
7. Depressed homemaker
8. Phone sex girl

because she "didn't have enough experience with cappuccino."

Carriage driver.
FOR THE ANIMAL-LOVING SLACKER WHO ENJOYS WEARING PERIOD ATTIRE AND LYING TO TOURISTS ABOUT INSIGNIFICANT CIVIC LANDMARKS.

Caterer.
EXPOSE YOURSELF TO SOME OF THE MORE INTOLERABLE ASPECTS OF ECO-NOMIC INJUSTICE AS RICH PEOPLE AMUSE THEMSELVES AND TALK LOUDLY ABOUT THEIR UPCOMING VACATIONS WHILE YOU RUN AROUND IN A SMELLY ILL-FITTING TUXEDO.

Coat-check girl.
The ultimate no-brainer.

Elementary school sub.
Can be quite lucrative in cities where the daily wage is augmented by combat pay.

Go Go dancer.
Self-objectification? Or simply a savvy economic move?

Grocery store checkout person.
WITH THE HELP OF THOSE CONVEYOR BELTS, LASER SCANNERS, AND AUTOMATIC CHANGE DISPENSERS, HERE YOU CAN COME SEDUCTIVELY CLOSE TO DOING NO ACTUAL WORK WHATSOEVER.

Health food store noontime sandwich delivery person.
Easy hours and crunchy clientele.

House painter.
Only for young, strapping, tan slackers who think their lives are still going someplace.

Ice-cream scooper.
Your forearm will swell like Popeye's and your friends will come visit you at work.

Lawn boy.
For the pathetic suburban slacker still residing at home with his parents.

Movie theater ticket person/usher.
For the aspiring *auteur*.

Night watchman/desk clerk.
For readers, writers, and people who can sleep with their eyes open.

Part-time telemarketer.
HOURS OF HOSTILE STRANGERS BERATING YOU FOR INTERRUPTING THEIR DINNERS WILL ADD TEXTURE AND DEPTH TO YOUR SLACK WELTANSCHAUUNG.

Photocopy shop worker.
Just how many frat party fliers can one man be expected to reproduce?

Pizza delivery person.
Every pizza you deliver is a piece of your own death.

Record store worker.
Sole job requirement: You must be demonstrably cooler than the people who come into the store.

Sous-chef.
Looks convincingly close to the first step on an actual career path.

Temp.
IDEAL FOR THE PARALEGAL WHO TUBES HER LSATS AND DECIDES TO FIGURE OUT WHAT SHE REALLY WANTS TO DO WITH HER LIFE. (LETHAL ONE-TWO PUNCH OF MANDATED PROMPTNESS AND ACCURATE TYPING IS TOO MUCH FOR MOST CAREER SLACKERS.)

Video store worker.
Watch movies at work! Provide your friends with free rentals!

Waiter.
Frankly, too much work for a lot of slackers. The ones who succeed in the business perfect their slouchy slo-mo service early on and never get alarmed by the weeds.

DREAM JOBS TO DAY JOBS

Match each dream job to the day job that would be the logical first step for a slacker attempting to scale the career ladder.

The Dream Jobs

1. Publisher, subversive national underground newspaper
2. Heir to Fellini's throne
3. Globe-trotting photojournalist
4. Lead vocalist, seminal Gothic metal band
5. Professional lottery winner
6. Childless housewife
7. Sidekick for late-night talk show host
8. Mayoral appointee to cushy do-nothing city job
9. Pulitzer Prize-winning novelist
10. Three-time Genius Grant winner

The Day Jobs

- [ ] a. Peddler, tie-dyed undershirts at Dead concerts
- [ ] b. Deputy Assistant Manager, Megaplex popcorn stand
- [ ] c. Guy who sells coverless paperbacks out of a grocery cart on street corners
- [ ] d. Comedy club cocktail waitress
- [ ] e. Part-time elementary school sub/noon aid
- [ ] f. Hot dog vendor merely a stone's throw from City Hall
- [ ] g. Freelance copy editor, dental office pamphlets
- [ ] h. Night watchman/occasional Bingo caller, local old folks' home
- [ ] i. Panhandler/petty thief
- [ ] j. Guy who sits in the Photomat booth

ANSWERS: 1g; 2b; 3j; 4a; 5h; 6e; 7d; 8f; 9c; 10i.

GUERILLA TEMPS UNITE

As far as gross exploitation of the labor force goes, it's hard to beat temporary employment. The temp agency charges, say, $12 an hour for your labor, of which they give you about $6 and keep the rest. The corporation pays the twelve bucks so it can avoid providing you with benefits such as health insurance and job security. As an added bonus, they are able to use you to illustrate a great economic truth to their beleaguered work force: Everyone is expendable.

Still, temp work is flexible and brainless, two qualities that don't exactly lack appeal. If you do decide to go the temp route, here are some things to keep in mind:

ORGANIZE A WORK SLOW-DOWN

If you are toiling away with a bunch of temps on a single job, convince the others to slow down to a snail's pace. This infuriates The Powers That Be, which serves them right for trying to exploit you.

Start Slow

When you get a new temp assignment, go through the initial training period exhibiting the sort of mental sharpness you would expect from someone missing a chromosome. This ensures low expectations on the part of your supervisors ("Now fold up the stack of paper and put it *in the envelope. . . .*") and guarantees you hours of slack time on the job.

Ambitious temps go to the other extreme, trying to be so competent and speedy that their supervisor will see the light and immediately hand them a full-time job. Alas, they are doing nothing but hastening their own obsolescence. The longer you can stretch out a job, the higher your dollar-per-task rate becomes.

Organize a Temp Sick Day

Get all the temps to call in sick on an important day of a time-sensitive project. If they don't want to give you job security, why should you give them labor security?

ONE WORD: SABOTAGE

If a temp job boss treats you badly enough, a little tampering with highly sensitive information might be in order. Consider rerouting significant documents from your mole's nest in the mail room or falling prey to a crippling bout of dyslexia while doing numerical data entry.

START TALKING "UNION"

An extremely effective way of causing problems that just so happens to be legal is to begin talking to your downtrodden coworkers about the tangible benefits of unionization. If you get fired for it, you can file charges with the National Labor Relations Board, and your employer will be forced to deal with a massive bureaucratic nightmare and piles of paperwork. You might come out with thousands of dollars of back pay, but even without it, you'll rest easier knowing that corporate America will think twice before trying to treat you like a meaningless cog in a machine designed to make rich people more money.

STEALING THINGS FROM WORK: SIN? OR PRACTICAL FORM OF POLITICAL PROTEST?

Stealing things from work is one profitable way to express your dissatisfaction with the status quo. Workplace theft is as American as bombing third-rate powers in order to increase our president's standing in popularity polls, though most people limit their pilfering to hand-held staplers and Post-It notes. Not so the slacker. Suppose you work in a restaurant. Depending on your individual management situation, your weekly take could include—and may not even be limited to—the following: food, alcohol, bottles of condiments, coffee, tea, sugar, packets of artificial sweetener, milk, juice, butter, salt and pepper shakers, dishrags, canisters of whipped cream, toilet paper, Kleenex, coffee filters, pots, soap, silverware, wineglasses, wine openers, coffee cups, plates, knives, cloth napkins, pens, candles, candle hold-

ers, ash trays, tables, chairs, fresh flowers, and matchbooks. But that's not all. The people upon whom you wait are bound to forget an umbrella every now and then. Or a pair of really cool sunglasses. Or maybe even a fancy silk scarf. And you remember what you learned in elementary school: finders keepers, losers place unfruitful telephone calls to the maitre d', who didn't see a thing. Should you happen to find yourself working for a caterer, you'll want to take home a souvenir from each grand home through which you tote hors d'oeuvres. The cautious might limit themselves to a handful of seashell-shaped soap from the bathroom or a knickknack whose disappearance from the guest bedroom is sure to be overlooked. But just think how swanky a crystal Tiffany ashtray would look on top of that coffee table you

discovered leaning against the curb on trash day. Imagine for a moment how far a pocket-sized Lalique figurine perched atop your $15 TV would go toward deconstructing the concept of wealth and privilege in America. And don't forget that bottles of wine and/or champagne can be wrapped in clothing and slipped into your backpack and are rarely missed. Sometimes a cruddy temp job is worth keeping for a while if only so you can maintain photocopying capabilities and access to a fax machine. Illegal use of the postage meter, free long-distance and international telephone calls, insider knowledge of Federal Express corporate account numbers—contemplating the possibilities of grunt-level office graft can be dizzying. Of course, you'll want to be sure to stock up on the usuals: pens, paper, scissors, sta-

plers, tape, tape dispensers, pencil holders, name plates of people you don't like, file folders, hanging files, envelopes of every imaginable dimension, paper clips, tacks, staples, staplers, index cards, and Post-It notes, as well as any card store gift mugs left unattended in the employee lunchroom. When you're not busy stealing things for yourself, you'll want to uncover ways to provide your slacker friends with things for free. You do this not only as an expedient means of combating economic injustice, but also because they'll undoubtedly hook you up as well. Before you know it, you'll have developed your own microeconomy based upon the bartering of goods stolen from your respective employers, and everyone's standard of living will dramatically increase.

The Sacking of a Slacker: Sleeping In Is the Best Revenge

DAY JOB:	REASON FOR TERMINATION:
Mini-mart register person	Malfunctioning snooze button
Shopping mall fudge crafter	Smirked during a managerial talking-to
House painter	Run-of-the-mill lax work ethic
Bellhop	Not quite obsequious enough
Deli cashier	Forgot to show up
Ice-cream scooper	Claimed to have "time to lean, not to clean"
BrobdingnagianPlex usher	Said the magic words: "Let's unionize!"
Bartender	Fell prey to trumped-up charge of gross insubordination
Waitress	Instigated massive back-of-the-house food fight
Fast food chef	Pulled housemate's truck up to Drive Thru window and loaded twelve boxes of frozen McNuggets into the cab while manager was locked in rest room

If the entrepreneurial spirit doesn't exactly shine forth from every slacker, in most of you it can be found some-

"I Ain't Gonna Work on Maggie's Farm No More": The Self-Employed Slacker

where, if only as a single glow-ing ember resting far beneath the dusty surface of your existence. Traditional slacker employment dreams—starting a found-object jewelry company, opening an anarchist book-store—have a distinct entrepreneurial edge. Unfortunately, getting in bed with, say, a Turkish cafe that you and your friend Alicia start up can all too quickly seem like a real job. Worse than a real job, because you'll undoubtedly be losing money hand over fist. But if you start small, with low or no over-head, you might be able to meet most (if not all) of your personal employment goals. That, and life would be much more predictable if you were the one in charge of firing you:

Law school application writer: You'll need a dose of writing talent and a lot of pathetic friends from college who are thinking about applying. When it comes to pricing: gouge 'em.

Pedicab Man: aka The Human Beast of Burden. Ideal for the slacker who wants to develop both thighs like tree trunks and a lifelong hatred of overweight tourists.

Photomemory Man: You need a Polaroid cam-era, some homemade cardboard frames, and a steady stream of gullible out-of-towners who will pay five bucks to have their picture taken with the Sears Tower looming in the back-ground.

Freelance proofreader: Requirements: Ph.D. in English literature and an ambitious first novel smoldering inside your Macintosh.

Housecleaner: Counterintuitive? Yes, but occa-sionally the slacker seeking self-employment will metamorphose into a Rent-a-Maid. Print up a couple of hundred fliers, don them rub-ber gloves, and practice saying, "I don't do windows."

Plant care technician/Professional dog-walker: Calls for a substantial degree of personal responsibility and an ability to walk around town with twelve dogs on leashes simultane-ously. Be forewarned, however: Neighborhood children will refer to you as "The Dog Man" for the rest of your life.

13 Things Parents Will Still Pay For

1. Collect calls
2. Catastrophic dental work
3. Nursing school
4. Mental health care
5. Kaplan
6. Annual Yuletide Greyhound tickets
7. Detox
8. Portable radiators
9. Law school application fees
10. Plane tickets back from Eastern Europe in the event of a counter-revolution
11. Bail
12. Transportation costs to and from relatives' funerals
13. Rehab

SLACKING ON THE DOLE: BILKING THE U.S. GOVERNMENT

The government has been kind enough to establish several generous programs that you can make use of to finance anything from an experimental first novel to a year-long TV binge. In all fairness, it should be noted that only a very small percentage of slackers do go ahead and make use of these handouts; most are stopped by ethics, the rest by logistics. Still, the Welfare Queen Slackers who manage to navigate the maze of red tape in order to liberate the cash that society owes them soon discover that sitting back and getting a check in the mail from Uncle Sam is much easier than waking up for even the best lousy day job.

UNEMPLOYMENT. UNEMPLOYMENT—THE GRANT YOU'VE ALWAYS DREAMED OF—IS BY FAR THE SLACK HANDOUT OF CHOICE. THE LENGTH OF YOUR STINT WILL DEPEND ON THE CURRENT UNEMPLOYMENT PERCENTAGE, AND IF YOU LOSE YOUR JOB AT THE RIGHT TIME YOU CAN CATCH THE CREST OF THE WAVE AND JUST KEEP RIDING, FOR FIFTY-TWO WEEKS PLUS A FOURTEEN-WEEK EXTENSION. GENERALLY, IT'S MORE LIKE TWENTY-SIX WEEKS PLUS A SEVEN-WEEK EXTENSION OR TWO, WHICH YOU GET IF YOU CAN PROVE THAT YOU'RE "UNEMPLOYABLE." IN ORDER TO BE ELIGIBLE FOR UNEMPLOYMENT YOU HAVE TO BE LAID OFF (YOU CAN'T BE FIRED OR SIMPLY QUIT), BUT SOME SYMPATHETIC EMPLOYERS WILL HELP YOU BEND THIS LITTLE RULE. IF YOU DECIDE TO DO THE UNEMPLOYMENT THING, FIND SOMEONE IN YOUR AREA WHO'S ALREADY SUCCESSFULLY RAKING IN HIS FELLOW TAXPAYERS' DOUGH, WHO WILL HELP WITH YOUR INITIATION, TELLING YOU THE BEST TIME TO SHOW UP AT THE UNEMPLOYMENT OFFICE AND LEADING YOU THROUGH THE PAPERWORK. THEN KICK BACK, PUT YOUR FEET UP, AND START THINKING UP A TITLE FOR YOUR WORK-IN-PROGRESS.

WELFARE. Welfare is a little more serious than unemployment, and the paperwork and hassles make it the choice of exceedingly few slackers. The welfare stigma still exists in the slack community, and lots of people who coast on unemployment refuse to take the logical next step, even if their novel is still in the embryonic stage after their first thirty-three weeks on the dole. Unlike unemployment, the welfare program makes use of "case workers," who are people who will pop in on you, unannounced, and proceed to get on your case. Again, though, if you are determined to do this, find a friend who is doing welfare in your state, and doing it well, to help you get started.

FOOD STAMPS. IF YOUR INCOME IS LOW ENOUGH, AND YOU CAN PROVE THAT MOST OF YOUR MONEY GOES TO RENT AND OTHER ESSENTIALS (NOT INCLUDING CONTROLLED SUBSTANCES), YOU MIGHT BE ELIGIBLE FOR FOOD STAMPS. YOU DON'T HAVE TO BE IRREDEEMABLY INDIGENT (ALTHOUGH IT HELPS)—YOU SIMPLY MUST PROVE THAT YOU ARE MAKING A GO AT SUPPORTING YOURSELF, BUT YOUR LOUSY FIVE-DOLLAR-AN-HOUR JOB MAKES IT IMPOSSIBLE FOR YOU TO AFFORD THE COLORFUL BREAKFAST CEREALS ASSOCIATED WITH TOUCAN SAM AND COUNT CHOCULA. WE CAN ALL SLEEP EASIER KNOWING THAT THIS IS STILL AN INALIENABLE RIGHT IN THIS GOD-FEARING COUNTRY OF OURS, AND THE GOVERNMENT WILL PROFFER THE HANDOUT NEEDED TO MAKE YOUR MORNING MEAL GREET YOU IN TECHNICOLOR.

HOW TO SELL LITTLE SNIPPETS OF YOUR LIVER FOR REALLY BIG BUCKS:
DRUG STUDY BONANZAS AND OTHER UNCONVENTIONAL WINDFALLS

For those of you who want to earn a great deal of money with an absolute minimum of time and effort, your options fall into the following categories: the unhealthy, the immoral, the unpleasant, and the illegal.

Not that that should dissuade you. If you already reside quite comfortably at the bottom of the health chain, what's a little radioactive material injected into your spleen to you, really, when it comes right down to it? And didn't you willfully defraud the Columbia House Record and Tape club in sixth grade? Several times? Until your parents caught you and made you rake neighborhood leaves to pay them back? And don't you still sign up, under ten assumed names, two months before you vacate any given apartment? I thought so.

Most of you probably have a fairly strict code of personal ethics that adheres to a Byzantine inner logic clear to no one but yourselves. For example, perhaps you give no second thought to milking the nation's entitlement system for all it's worth, yet you refuse to perpetrate

even the most minor insurance scam. Or maybe you find the thought of taking an unemployment check repugnant, but you would gladly defraud the government by "marrying" a foreigner, and you've spent years toiling away in the underground economy. Perhaps you see nothing wrong with instigating a nuisance lawsuit every now and then, but you're loath to sell your genomes to strangers.

Alas, in this as in everything else it's up to you to follow your own slightly skewed moral compass. Please keep in mind that the reporting of this information does not constitute an endorsement of any illegal activity contained herein, and neither this author nor Warner Books nor the massive, bloated Time Warner media conglomeration would ever encourage or instruct an individual or group thereof to break any local, state, or federal laws:

THE DRUG STUDY

THE WORLD OF THE PERENNIAL DRUG STUDY PARTICIPANT IS AS BLEAK, HUMORLESS, AND DOG-EAT-DOG AS THAT OF ANY WALL STREET MARAUDER. IT TAKES A CERTAIN AMOUNT OF DESPERATION TO INGEST EXPERIMENTAL PHARMACEUTICALS FOR A LIVING, AND IN ORDER TO MAKE ANY SERIOUS CASH AT IT YOU'LL NEED FLEXIBILITY IN YOUR SCHEDULE, A CAVALIER ATTITUDE TOWARD YOUR PHYSICAL WELL-BEING, AND A WILLINGNESS TO WALK AROUND WITH PATCHES OF GAUZE TAPED TO YOUR ARMS FOR WEEKS AT A TIME.

$200 AND UP

UNFORTUNATELY, MOST DRUG STUDIES CALL FOR "HEALTHY MEN AGED 18-35," SO YOU LADIES GET THE SHORT END OF THE STICK ON THIS ONE. (BE SURE TO READ THE FINE PRINT, LEST YOUR SPERM STOP SWIMMING INDEFINITELY.)

THE DRUG STUDY — VARIES

THIS ONE'S A GEM THAT'S AS BEAUTIFUL AS IT IS RARE, BUT MOST UNIVERSITIES HARBOR AT LEAST ONE RENEGADE PROF WHO IS ANXIOUS TO STUDY THE SHORT-TERM EFFECTS OF LSD ON BASIC MATH SKILLS. LIE ON THE APPLICATION FORM IF YOU MUST, AS WHAT YOU BLITHELY CONSIDER "OCCASIONAL RECREATIONAL DRUG USE" WILL PROBABLY BE REGARDED BY THEM AS "ADDICTION."

The Sleep Deprivation Study — SEVERAL HUNDRED

One of the many types of studies that you can hook up with at your local university's psych department, the sleep deprivation study is a lucrative classic that will fuel cocktail-party conversations well into your "occasional hemorrhoidal flare-up" years. Still, sleep is such a precious commodity that the thought of giving it up, even temporarily, is difficult for most slackers to stomach. The payment for psych studies varies, and it is based primarily on whether or not they have to lock you up for a period of time in order to study you. A good, profitable study will inconvenience you for a week or so but render no lasting physical or psychological scars.

PLASMA PEDDLING — VARIES, BUT NOT TOO MUCH

YOU'RE NEVER GOING TO GET RICH SELLING YOUR PLASMA, BUT THERE ARE ONLY SO MANY TIMES YOU CAN LIQUIDATE YOUR HOUSEMATE'S CD COLLECTION, AND YOU *DO* HAVE TO EAT. IDEALLY YOU'LL GET ON THE PLASMA SELLING CIRCUIT AND BE ABLE TO RETURN TO THE CENTER AT REGULARLY SCHEDULED INTERVALS TO SELL YOUR PLASMA AND PARTAKE OF THEIR BOUNTIFUL SUPPLY OF FREE COOKIES AND ORANGE JUICE.

The Selling of One's Eggs — VARIES, BUT EASILY OVER $1000

While hocking sperm is not particularly lucrative, if you permit a surgeon to slice you open and remove a handful of your *eggs*, you're in gravy. Selling your eggs is not only profitable, it's noble, which is a rare and compelling combination. The potential downsides, obviously, are substantial (bodily harm and possible death, mangled reproductive organs, children with your glittering sense of humor dotting the globe and eventually, unknowingly, intermarrying . . .)

The Green-Card Wedding — $3,000-$10,000

PARTICULARLY POPULAR AROUND UNIVERSITIES WITH A BIG INTERNATIONAL STUDENT POPULATION, MOST GREEN-CARD WEDDINGS LINK WEALTHY YOUNG FOREIGN GENTLEMEN WITH SLACKER CHICKS IN DIRE NEED OF A FEW GRAND TO TIDE THEM OVER WHILE THEY PAINT. YOU MUST REMAIN LEGALLY AND CONVINCINGLY MARRIED FOR TWO YEARS, AFTER WHICH YOU CAN DIVORCE AT YOUR LEISURE.

THE INSURANCE SCAM — Varies

SAY YOU BUY AN EXPENSIVE NEW BIKE. A BIKE THAT YOU PUT ON YOUR CREDIT CARD, THE ONE WITH THE PURCHASE PROTECTION PLAN THAT THEY GAVE YOU BACK WHEN YOU WERE IN COLLEGE AND DEEMED AN ACCEPTABLE CREDIT RISK. SUPPOSE AFTER TWO OR THREE WEEKS YOU WALK OUTSIDE A BOOKSTORE AND DISCOVER THAT *YOUR NEW BIKE HAS BEEN STOLEN*. YOU FILE A POLICE REPORT, SUBMIT IT TO THE CREDIT CARD COMPANY, AND THEN—PRESTO— BOTH YOU AND YOUR FRIEND TED HAVE EXPENSIVE NEW BIKES.

The Nuisance Lawsuit
varies, but possibly huge

THE NUISANCE LAWSUIT CAN CALL FOR MORE EFFORT AND SUBTERFUGE THAN THE AVERAGE SLACKER IS WILLING TO INVEST, BUT THE RETURNS, AS YOU CAN WELL IMAGINE, CAN BE LIKE WINNING THE LOTTERY. WHEN YOU STUMBLE UPON SOMETHING THAT LOOKS SUSPICIOUSLY LIKE AN OPPORTUNITY, GO AHEAD AND SEIZE IT. THEN SEEK OUT JUST THE RIGHT AMBULANCE-CHASING LAWYER WITH A FONDNESS FOR CONTINGENCY FEES AND A PENCHANT FOR SETTLING OUT OF COURT, AND BEFORE YOU KNOW IT YOU'LL BE COMPARING TAX SHELTER SCAMS WITH YOUR NEW FRIENDS, THE IDLE RICH.

Forewarned Is Forearmed

Slacker A and Slacker B were close friends. Slacker A had health insurance, due to his position as a serving professional with a nationally franchised restaurant chain specializing in potato skins and buffalo wings. Slacker B—a part-time register person at a hole-in-the-wall record exchange—did not. When Slacker B seriously injured himself in a freak skateboarding accident for which he was entirely at fault and unable to sue anyone, Slacker A allowed him to check into a local hospital under an assumed identity, namely, his own. Thus Slacker B, posing as Slacker A, received over two weeks' worth of hospital care, which was generously paid for by the insurance company of Slacker A. While his friend was laid up in the hospital, Slacker A dutifully showed up for each and every shift at work. Little did he know that those days of toting potato skins and buffalo wings to overweight strangers would seal his fate. When the insurance company, the hospital, and the restaurant franchise got around to comparing notes, Slackers A and B were introduced to levels of the criminal justice system that they had heretofore left unexplored as they discovered the true meaning behind the phrase "federal offense."

RATE YOUR DAY JOB

Quiz #2

Inching up the wage scale is important, but one should never underestimate the importance of finding a day job that truly suits the slack lifestyle. Before you leave your $6-an-hour job managing that tiny out-of-the-way used bookstore for a $14-an-hour job toting cement blocks around a construction site, take some time to assess those intangibles that make a day job worth keeping:

"I never have to wake up before 11:00 A.M. to make it to work on time."

TRUE	4 points
FALSE	-3 points

"I work three days a week or fewer."

TRUE	5 points
FALSE	-2 points

"My job taxes less than 2 percent of my mental reserves."
                    TRUE   4 points
                    FALSE   -2 points

"I can read books and magazines of my own selection while at work."
                    TRUE   2 points
                    ·FALSE   -1 point

"I can watch television while at work."
                    TRUE   3 points
                    FALSE   -0 points

"My friends and acquaintances can come to my place of employment and talk to me for hours while I continue to receive pay."
                    TRUE   2 points
                    FALSE   -2 points

"I have never broken a sweat while at work."
                    TRUE   2 points
                    FALSE   -2 points

"I never have to move quickly while at work."
                    TRUE   3 points
                    FALSE   -2 points

"I would categorize my stress level while at work as 'low' to 'extremely low.' "
                    TRUE   4 points
                    FALSE   -2 points

"I can make long, involved telephone calls of a personal nature while on the job."
                    TRUE   1 point
                    FALSE   -1 point

"I can make long, involved long-distance telephone calls of a personal nature while on the job."
                    TRUE   2 points
                    FALSE   0 points

"I can make long, involved international telephone calls of a personal nature while on the job."
                    TRUE   3 points
                    FALSE   0 points

"I am free to be sullen and rude to the people I come into contact with while on the job."
                    TRUE   2 points
                    FALSE   -1 point

"I can more or less choose to work whenever the mood strikes."
                    TRUE   4 points
                    FALSE   -1 point

"I can smoke while on the job."
                    TRUE   2 points
                    FALSE   -5 points

"I am *encouraged* to smoke on the job."
                    TRUE   4 points
                    FALSE   0 points

"I have access to an unlimited supply of free coffee while at work."
                    TRUE   4 points
                    FALSE   -2 points

"I can successfully perform the duties of my job while hung over."
                    TRUE   1 point
                    FALSE   -1 point

"I can successfully perform the duties of my job while intoxicated."
                    TRUE   3 points
                    FALSE   0 points

"I can successfully perform the duties of my job while under the influence of mind-altering drugs."
                    TRUE   4 points
                    FALSE   0 points

"I can drink on the job with impunity."
                    TRUE   2 points
                    FALSE   0 points

"When I elect not to show up for work as scheduled, I am not promptly fired."
                    TRUE   3 points
                    FALSE   -2 points

"When I elect not to show up for work as scheduled, I am neither reprimanded nor promptly fired."
                    TRUE   5 points
                    FALSE   0 points

"I would have little or no trouble leaving my job for a period of several months and then returning to it."
                    TRUE   3 points
                    FALSE   -2 points

"I do not have to wear a uniform to work."
                    TRUE   1 point
                    FALSE   -4 points

"I do not have to wear a funny hat to work."
                    TRUE   0 points
                    FALSE   -6 points

"I never wear a suit to work." (men only)
> TRUE   0 points
> FALSE   -10 points

"I never wear panty hose and high heels to work." (women only)
> TRUE   0 points
> FALSE   -5 points

"My parents are ashamed to tell their friends what I do for a living."
> TRUE   7 points
> FALSE   -1 point

"I can sit down with my friends, smoke, talk, read, write, doodle, put my feet up, and drink coffee for prolonged periods of time while still getting paid at work."
> TRUE   10 points
> FALSE   -3 points

• •

SCORING:

-60 to -1 points: YOUR DAY JOB SELECTION INSTINCT IS *SEVERELY* IMPAIRED. THE ONLY WAY YOUR SCORE WOULD BE ACCEPTABLE FOR A SLACKER IS IF YOUR SALARY IS ENABLING YOU TO SOCK AWAY ENOUGH MONEY TO RETIRE WITHIN THE MONTH. OTHERWISE, DO YOURSELF A FAVOR. GET A NEW JOB.

0 to 19 points: YOUR SCORE PUTS YOU IN THAT SLACK EMPLOYMENT LIMBO THAT INDICATES THAT YOU JUST AREN'T TRYING HARD ENOUGH. LEARN TO TEND BAR, FOR HEAVEN SAKES. BONE UP ON YOUR CAPPUCCINO SKILLS, PERFECT THAT SNARL, AND GO APPLY AT YOUR NEIGHBORHOOD CAFE. TRUST ME, YOU'RE WORKING TOO HARD.

20 to 50 points: YOUR SCORE, WHILE EMINENTLY RESPECTABLE, STILL LEAVES AMPLE ROOM FOR IMPROVEMENT. THE QUESTION YOU MUST NOW PONDER IS SIMPLE: DO I HAVE MY JOB, OR DOES MY JOB HAVE ME?

50+ POINTS: CONGRATULATIONS!

YOU HAVE MASTERED THE MOST IMPORTANT ASPECT OF SLACK LIVING. YOU HAVE FOUND THE PERFECT DAY JOB. (NOW, TRY YOUR BEST NOT TO GET CANNED.)

THE LOOK
AND
HOW TO GET IT

PRINCIPLES OF SLACK FASHION

Even though you like to think that you exist outside the realm of middle-class concerns, slackers do not remain wholly untouched by the vagaries of fashion. A sudden longing for the Seventies on New York runways will eventually find its way to the cafe, in the shape of a waifish girl wearing a threadbare T-shirt with an iron-on photo of Farrah on her chest. Yet somehow the slacker fashion netherworld—where old clothes go to die before they become "vintage"—retains an almost timeless quality, based upon a consistent application of the slacker's sartorial philosophy.

Some people will undoubtedly claim there *are* no rules—that nonconformity is just that—and everyone is parading around in gray mechanics' uniforms with the name Ed embroidered on their chests because they want to. Perhaps. But the following few principles govern even the most outré of the slacker's fashoin choices:

APATHY

The slacker doesn't care if there is a hole the size of an Egg McMuffin in the armpit of his sweater. He doesn't care if the shirt he has on is two sizes too small, or if the jacket he has on is four sizes too big. He doesn't care if his socks are mismatched, if his T-shirt is on inside out, or if his jeans are so crispy that they stand at attention in the corner of his bedroom.

ECONOMY

Even an egregious fashion faux pas can be forgiven if it is committed in the name of economy. Silver duct tape wrapped around a pair of black boots is A-OK, as is an ugly overcoat as long as it was unearthed from a neighborhood garbage can. Slackers respect a healthy disregard for gainful employment even more than style, and they are tolerant of the kinds of compromises that must accompany poverty.

PROXIMITY

While not always apparent to the casual onlooker, most of the slacker's fashion decisions are based on nothing more than the location of various elements of his wardrobe as he dresses for the upcoming day. A pair of jeans hanging from the doorknob is more likely to be worn than an identical pair that happens to be folded up in a dresser drawer, just as the socks on the kitchen floor will stay there until his feet get cold while he's heating up some ramen.

A BRIEF HISTORY OF THE GOATEE

1601-1643 Reign and Life of Louis XIII, King of France, and the Daddy-O of the Goatee. Short pointed beards were the height of fashion under Le Roi Louis, who was described as high-strung, over-intellectualizing (Richelieu wrote of him in *Testament Politique,* "Your Majesty's mind rules your body so completely that the slightest excess of emotion affects your heart and reacts upon your whole organism."), and perpetually miserable, a description that befits the modern-day cafe-dweller after the fourth or fifth latte.

1585-1642 Life of Cardinal Richelieu. Chief minister under Louis XIII, the good Cardinal basically ran the show. From his initial service to the King in 1624 until his death eighteen years later he dominated the country of France and allowed no political changes to occur in all of Europe without some measure of his control and influence. A literary snob, he founded the snooty-to-this-day Académie Française in 1635. Ruthless, arrogant, and a genius, political and otherwise, Richelieu also had an oft-remarked-upon fondness for cats that apparently approached the bizarre. French fashion influence being what it was and is, the short pointed beard was copied the Western world over, appearing on all courtiers, aristocrats, and dandies, including Charles I (1600-1649), King of England, who unfortunately lost both his goatee and head on the block in 1649, and Gustavus Adolphus (alias the "Snow King," 1594-1632), the great general and king of Sweden.

REPETITION

ACTUALLY NOTHING MORE THAN A BY-PRODUCT OF THE THREE PRINCIPLES OUTLINED ABOVE, SLACKERS TEND TO WEAR THE SAME FEW ARTICLES OF CLOTHING OVER AND OVER AGAIN. VIOLATING THE ONE THING WE ALL LEARNED IN ELEMENTARY SCHOOL, THE TRUE SLACKER SEES NOTHING WRONG WITH WEARING THE SAME SHIRT, DAY AFTER DAY, WEEK IN, WEEK OUT, UNTIL EITHER THE SEASON CHANGES OR ENOUGH PEOPLE TELL HIM IT OUGHT TO BE WASHED. THUS, IT'S POSSIBLE TO IDENTIFY A PARTICULAR PERSON WITHIN A CERTAIN SLACKER SET WITH A TAG LIKE "THE GUY WHO WEARS THAT BLUE T-SHIRT," WHEN "THE WEIRDO WITH THE SPARSE GOA-TEE" OR "THAT DUDE WHO'S FINISH-ING UP HIS PHILOSOPHY DISSERTATION" COULD SIG-NIFY ANY ONE OF SEVERAL INDIVIDUALS.

UTILITY

From the skillful appli-cation of safety pins to near total disregard for holes, stains, and smells, the slacker wants his clothes to clothe him, not much more. He chooses ensembles whose day-to-night transition is effortless: outfits that can take him from his job at the cafe to his afternoon chess game at another cafe to his evening of crafting poems at another cafe. His fashion watchword: Functionality.

INATTENTION TO FIGURE FLAWS

THE SORT OF CAMOUFLAGE THAT IS TAUGHT TO YOUNG WOMEN BY *GLAMOUR* MAGAZINE'S FASHION DOS AND DON'TS IS ALMOST ENTIRELY ABSENT WITHIN THE SLACKING SUB-CULTURE. SOME MIGHT SUGGEST THAT IT IS SORELY MISSED. HIPS SWATHED IN LAYERS OF PLAID FLANNEL, INAP-PROPRIATELY COLORED BRASSIERES MAKING THEIR PRESENCE KNOWN BENEATH FRUIT OF THE LOOM UNDER-SHIRTS, FLESHY TATTOOED UPPER ARMS OOZING OUT OF SLEEVELESS MOCK TURTLENECKS . . .

SECRETS OF OUTPATIENT HAIR: HOW TO LOOK FUNCTIONALLY INSANE

- Go platinum!
- Trim your bangs with steak knife
- Ask your hairdresser for a Dorothy Hamill
- In a demonstration of solidarity with your international pot-smoking brethren, start cultivating dreads
- Two words: Hat hair
- Submit to angry drunken girlfriend armed with pinking shears

IRONY

The slacker's exis-tence is lent texture

and meaning by his heightened sense of irony. So, too, is his wardrobe. A pair of Calvin Klein jeans he finds for fifty cents at a porch sale are more than just a great deal—they are the screams of a thousand peasants threatening the peace and quiet of the king. Designer labels, brand names, T-shirts designed to encourage consumption of nostalgio-popular snack foods, *H. R. Puff-n-Stuff* lunchboxes, hats with ear flaps, Blue Light Specials—the neat thing about irony, you must admit, is that at this point just about anything can be pressed into service.

IF IT'S NOT FREE YOU CAN'T AFFORD IT:
THE LOOK FOR MEN

AS MUCH AS YOUR DISTINCT PERSONAL STYLE IS A BY-PRODUCT OF YOUR BLINDING ORIGINALITY AND UNBRIDLED GENIUS, IF YOU'LL TAKE A MOMENT TO LOOK AROUND YOU YOU'LL REALIZE THAT EVERYONE YOU KNOW DRESSES EXACTLY THE SAME WAY. ALL OF YOUR FRIENDS AT THE CAFE. THAT DUDE WHO WORKS AT THE PHOTOCOPY PLACE. EVEN THOSE LOSERS IN THE BUD COMMERCIALS. BUT DON'T LET THAT STOP YOU FROM DRESSING EXACTLY THE WAY YOU WANT. YOU CAN'T HELP IT IF YOU'RE A TRENDSETTER. YOU CAN'T HELP IT IF EVERYONE COPIED YOU.

1. Untuck everything.

Your free-flowing shirt is a shining symbol of your total disregard for the restricting elements of uptight bourgeois culture. You're suddenly underdressed for every occasion. Tuck only when you are trying to "pass"; say, if you're attempting to infiltrate an invite-only wine and

cheese affair at an exclusive gallery downtown.

2. Don't wear a watch.

THE ULTIMATE SLACKER NON-ACCESSORY, THE ABSENT WATCH SYMBOLIZES BOTH YOUR FRUGALITY AND YOUR STYLISH INDIFFERENCE TOWARD TIME. THE WATCHLESS WRIST SUGGESTS THAT YOUR LIFE IS YOUR OWN, THAT YOU NEVER HAVE TO BE ANYPLACE BY A PREDETERMINED HOUR, AND THAT YOU HAVE NOTHING BUT CONTEMPT FOR THE WESTERN WORLD'S CLOCK-PUNCHING WORK ETHIC.

3. Wear a hat.

Not only can a hat enable you to cut down on time-consuming bathing, the

INSIDE THE SLACK POCKET
- money machine card
- money machine slip, denying the availability of funds
- cigarettes (hard pack)
- 7-Eleven matchbook, filled with damp matches
- tiny globe key chain with screwdriver/bottle-opener attachment, containing nine keys, including those from last three apartments and parents' house.
- $4.87
- losing lotto ticket
- red cocktail napkin with the words "great 1st nov'l idea: *desire*" scrawled across it in black ink
- partially-popped kernel of popcorn
- bus token
- broken pencil
- lint

right one can help you eliminate it altogether. But be careful, as even the most innocent ember of creativity can easily spark a towering inferno atop your head. While the wild impulse that

causes you to slap down $6.50 for a fez reminiscent of Mr. Cunningham is fine, the urge to wear it to your sister's wedding should probably be squelched.

4. Accessorize with care.

SCARF. SILVER DEATH'S-HEAD RING. ANTIQUE MONOCLE DANGLING FROM A BLACK SHOELACE AROUND YOUR NECK. THE SLACK LOOK IS NEVER FUSSY, NEVER OVERLY ORNATE, BUT A SINGLE WELL-CHOSEN WARDROBE ELEMENT THAT DOUBLES AS A TALISMAN IS QUINTESSENTIALLY SLACK.

5. Cultivate your facial hair.

Alas, the goatee lives on. Since it has passed from slack culture into mainstream culture, from Austin to Boise to the outskirts of even the smallest obscure Canadian hamlet, the true slacker must now perform the dreaded task of *shaving it off*. The same people who were wearing ponytails in the late Eighties—paunchy self-satisfied New York advertising account executives, mainly—are now wearing goatees. Go on, *try something else*.

6. Layering is everything.

JUST REMEMBER THAT THERE IS NO LIMIT TO THE AMOUNT OF CLOTHING YOU CAN DRAPE OVER YOUR FRAME, AND THE THREE LAYERS CLOSEST TO YOUR SKIN NEED NEVER BE LAUNDERED. YOU'LL KNOW YOU'VE GOT IT RIGHT IF A WALK TO THE 7-ELEVEN IN FEBRUARY MAKES YOU FEEL LIKE A BRONTASAURUS OUT ON A CASUAL STROLL THROUGH LA BREA.

1883-1924 Yet Another Black Date in Goatee History: Franz Kafka brooded, wrote, and flirted with socialism all over the cafes of Prague and Berlin. Oddly enough, he lived and died clean-shaven.

1868-1963 Life of W.E.B. DuBois. The goatee has been recognized as a favorite of the stylish African-American gent, and its practitioners span the decades, including DuBois, James Pierson Beckworth, Robert Smalls, Maulana Karenga, Imamu Amiri Baraka, and modern-day Black Pack power broker Spike Lee.

1870-1924 Life of Nikolai Lenin. Became head of Russian State in 1917. Father of the twentieth-century goatee and, coincidentally enough, twentieth-century communism as well. Really quite a celeb in his own right. He came from, *quelle* surprise, a fabulously bourgeois background—just like yours.

THE SLACK LOOK FOR WOMEN IS NOT AS CODIFIED AS THE LOOK FOR MEN. THE FEMALE SUBCULTURE HAS BEEN SO TAINTED BY ITS EXPOSURE TO QUASI-SLACK ELEMENTS—ART SCHOOL CHICKS IN BLACK CAT SUITS AND DECISIVELY CUT HAIR, EARTH-MOTHER VEGANS WEARING FLOWING SKIRTS AND FELT CLOGS—THAT EVEN THE MOST DISCERNING OF YOU LADY SLACKERS MIGHT START TO THINK THAT ANYTHING GOES.

AND UP TO A POINT YOU'D BE RIGHT. BUT KEEP IN MIND THE FOLLOWING BASICS, AND THEN LET YOUR IRREPRESSIBLE SPIRIT RUN FREE:

1. Untuck everything.

Even the most put-together ensemble will suddenly smack of slack if the shirttails are left dangling and the sweater droops down around your hips. You were smart enough to stop reading *Seventeen* at fourteen, *Glamour* at fifteen, and *Cosmo* at sixteen—why start listening to them now?

2. Easy on the make-up.

IF YOU PAY TOO MUCH ATTENTION TO YOUR LIPSTICK, YOU'LL QUICKLY BE MISTAKEN FOR AN ART SCHOOL CHICK OR A SUBURBAN HIGH SCHOOL POSER AND HAVE TO PUT UP WITH ALL SORTS OF TESTOSTERONE-FUELED STUPIDITY FOISTED UPON YOU BY YOUR SLACK BROTHERS-IN-ARMS. MAKE-UP, IF WORN AT ALL, SHOULD BE SOMETHING OF AN AFTERTHOUGHT, APPLIED BUT NEVER REAPPLIED, SUGGESTING YOU HAVE MORE IMPORTANT THINGS TO DO WITH YOUR TIME THAN POWDER YOUR NOSE.

3. Steal your boyfriend's clothes.

You must go about collecting clothes from the men you date with the sort of intense bloodlust that we now associate with politically insensitive portrayals of Native Americans stalking for scalps. Take no prisoners. Alas, there is nothing better than a nice Brooks Brothers buttondown, lifted after two evenings with a plodding accountant who paid for dinner *and* movie *and* popcorn but had never even heard of Christina Rossetti.

4. Have fun with your footwear.

Shoes are important, and if you can give the impression that your shoes originated as part of a totally different outfit than the one you happen to be wearing, you're on the right track. Choose the right kind of industrial footwear and you'll seem serious and no-nonsense, as even the most flowery trapeze dress can be sobered up by a pair of beat-up black combat boots.

5. Layering is everything.

Less important in the summer months, layering is an extremely cost-efficient way of cold-weather dressing. Tights and thermals can make even the lightest cotton skirt suddenly a year-round staple,

> **WHY WE'VE STOPPED WEARING UNDERPANTS**
> -Takes less time to get dressed.
> -Takes less time to get undressed.
> -No unsightly panty lines to mar our fashion silhouettes.
> -Makes us feel like rock stars.
> -Form of quiet rebellion against intolerable bourgeois mores.
> -The thought of buying used underwear from a thrift store grosses even us out.

and a T-shirt, long underwear top, and two flannels equal one outrageously expensive J. Crew wool sweater.

1879-1940 Life of Leon Trotsky. Another important communist who sported a goatee. Attacked by Stalin after Lenin's death in 1924, Trotsky was exiled in 1927 and eventually was killed with an ice-pick through the skull. Stalin (1879-1953) took over from Lenin as ruler of the Soviet Union in 1927. Loved, hated, and feared, he was responsible for the deaths of tens of thousands of his own people; however, he wore a big, fat, stupid mustache.

1956 Allen Ginsberg published *Howl*.

1948 Jack Kerouac began writing *On the Road*. The Beat Movement in America had begun.

1957 In a burst of Benzedrine-induced frenzy, Kerouac finally finished his masterpiece, nine years after he started it. Get a job, man!

Mid-1950s-1960s American Beatnik Coffeehouse Movement. A lot of educated boys moved to New York and San Francisco, wore black, smoked cigarettes, drank coffee, composed poetry of questionable value, had their friends accompany the readings of it with bongos while their girlfriends did interpretive dances, and, oh yes, worked on their goatees. Bob Dylan had one, and so should you.

EVEN IF THE SLACK FASHION DIRECTIVE SEEMS TO MAKE ROOM FOR WIDE VARIATIONS IN TASTE AND PERSONAL STYLE, FIGURING OUT WHERE TO BUY YOUR CLOTHES IS NOT AS EASY AS IT MIGHT SEEM.

A GOOD RULE OF THUMB IS THAT IF YOU DON'T FEEL COMPELLED TO LAUNDER A NEW ACQUISITION BEFORE YOU WEAR IT, IT'S PROBABLY OUT OF YOUR PRICE RANGE.

THE MORE SUSPECT, PAWED-OVER, THIRDHAND, AND POTENTIALLY SOCIAL-DISEASE-RIDDEN A GIVEN ARTICLE OF CLOTHING IS, THE BETTER.

A DISTINCTION MUST BE MADE BETWEEN THE STORES YOU BROWSE THROUGH AND THE PLACES WHERE YOU ACTUALLY BUY THINGS. YOU MIGHT LOOK LOVINGLY AT THAT NEW SCOOP-NECKED, CRUMPLED POLYESTER, CALF-LENGTH FLOWERY DRESS HANGING IN THE WINDOW OF URBAN OUTFITTERS, BUT WHERE ARE YOU GOING TO GET YOUR HANDS ON NINETY BUCKS? THE GAP, OF COURSE, EXISTS AS AN OBJECT OF MOCKERY AND NOTHING ELSE, AND THE FACT THAT THEY PUT JACK KEROUAC IN THEIR ADS ONLY FUELS THE FIRE OF SLACKER CONTEMPT.

THRIFT STORES.

Thrift stores come in two varieties: urban and suburban. You will unfortunately have to make do with urban most of the time, unless you have a friend with a car, in which case make it your business to drive into the land of the manicured lawns and get

some dry-clean-only secondhand clothes with that timeless designer label appeal.

K-MART.

Shopping at K-Mart—not simply hightailing it to the shampoo section to buy a gallon of Suave for ninety-nine cents, but marching into the dressing room carrying an arm full of clothes dangling Jaclyn Smith tags—signifies a signifi-

THE GAP: OUT OF YOUR PRICE RANGE

cant coming of age for the novice slacker, in which that upper-middle-class suburban high school mentality is skewered and (momentarily) left for dead.

MILITARY SURPLUS STORES.

The surplus store doesn't just mean snow fatigues and mosquito netting

anymore, and if you happen upon a cheap mock-military surplus store (all the ambiance of the original, but with racks of flannel shirts and piles of outdated Swedish Navy regalia), you're in for a day of one-stop slack shopping.

STOLEN /FOUND CLOTHES.

The best kind of cheap clothing is free clothing. By far. From the T-shirts you steal from your boyfriend to the bowling shoes you find in the garbage can, the rule is that if you can steal it or find it, don't buy it.

CHURCH RUMMAGE SALES.

Basically, if a guy has died and he's your size, you're in clover.

YARD SALES,

Depending on where you live, yard sales run the

gamut from white trash setting out broken knickknacks on card tables to white trash dangling faded clothes on wire hangers from laundry lines. But since everything is priced at fifty cents, and even that's negotiable, the yard sale remains a key slack shopping opportunity.

Garage Sales.
Like a yard sale, but one that takes place in a garage.

Carport Sales.
Another name for a garage sale.

Porch Sales.
A yard sale that takes place below the Mason-Dixon line.

Sidewalk Sales.
The urban apartment dweller's answer to sales of the Yard, Garage, Carport, and Porch variety. Throwing one is a traditional slack rite of passage, marking your earliest attempts to liquidate your possessions to raise funds for that hoped-for trip to Belize. Brace yourself, though: Random passersby will act as if your cherished belongings were radioactive and will look upon you with undisguised disgust.

1959-1963 The goatee made its debut in mass popular culture in the form of Maynard G. Krebs, the bongo-beating, job-fearing, sort of dirty beatnik who was Dobie's best friend on the very popular television show *The Many Loves of Dobie Gillis*. Maynard was played by *Gilligan's Island* Bob Denver. Basically, for four years Maynard and Dobie attempted to decide something about their futures. (The original Beavis and Butthead, Wayne and Garth, Bill and Ted, ad infinitum.)

October 21, 1969 Black Date in Goatee History: A bloated, as always clean-shaven Kerouac died in an alcoholic stupor, having lived the past three years of his life in his mom's house.

1970s Black Decade in Goatee History. Everyone got really hairy.

1971 Bob Denver arrested for possession of narcotics paraphernalia.

1985 Black Date in Goatee History. In an ill-fated attempt to hide from the world the fact that he wore peach shirts with white suits, Don Johnson—star of popular TV preen/Phil Collins fest *Miami Vice*—grew a strange stubble and left it there. Pop sensation and WHAM!-escapee George Michael followed suit. The age of sculpted scruff had begun.

TRANSCENDING HYGIENE: GRUNGE WAS A TREND, GREASE IS A LIFESTYLE

Level	Occasion	Action
1	The Lost Weekend	↓→ -Pick crusty scum out of corner of eyes
2	Not going home for the holidays	↓→ -Wipe dried saliva off of cheek
3	Contemplating suicide	↓→ -Singe off unwanted body hair with stray menthol cigarette butt
4	Starting the bender	↓→ -Don pair of "air-cleaned" underwear hanging from doorknob
5	Joni Loves Chachi marathon on cable	↓→ -Don pair of "air-cleaned" underwear hanging from doorknob, but turn them inside out
6	Visiting the unemployment office	↓→ -Scrape teeth with uncut fingernails wihle
7	In the middle of a powerful new short story	↓→ -Elect to cultivate facial hair in order to camouflage embarrassing adult-onset acne
8	Heading to work	↓→ -Undergo cursory "trust, but verify" underarm inspection
9	Sliding-scale therapy appointment	↓→ -Brush teeth (without toothpaste)
10	Crashing a bar mitzvah for free alcohol	↓→ -Brush teeth (with stolen toothpaste)
11	Important job interview	↓→ -Run fingers through hair
12	Coffee with old girlfriend	↓→ -Fumigate private parts with pine-based air freshener
13	Reading poems at an open mike night	↓→ -Steal roommate's fresh socks
14	Hot date	↓→ -Inspect self-inflicted nose piercing for signs of infection
15	Stint as a nude model for housemate's art class	↓→ -Manually de-lint belly button
16	Stepsister's wedding	↓→ -Shower
17	Posing for band photo	↓→ -Trim goatee
18	Dinner with generous visiting grandparents	→ -Launder jeans

Summer 1989 Richard Linklater began shooting the seminal film *Slacker* in Austin, Texas. A total of ten—over 20 percent—of the men in the film sported goatees.

1992 Nirvana's Nevermind album released. The single "Smells Like Teen Spirit" went to number one on the *Billboard* chart. Grunge descended upon America. "Alternative" became not so much so. Every hip young rocker or Hollywood star sported a goatee. Kurt Cobain did, as did that silly guy from Stone Temple Pilots; however, that other grunge-maestro, Eddie Vedder of Pearl Jam, remained, for a while at least, clean-shaven (presumably because he was the best-looking of the lot and had nothing to hide). Matt Dillon's character in the movie *Singles* (a character based on Pearl Jam's guitarist Jeff Ament) sported a goatee. Members of Pearl Jam played his bandmates in the movie.

25 October 1993 *People Weekly* released its annual "Best and Worst Dressed" issue, with a special report entitled "Follicles of '93: The Goatee is Back." So, who

1992-1994 Evan Dando of The Lemonheads appeared on some twenty magazine covers, was widely heralded as the Fabio of College Rock, and yet REMAINED CLEAN SHAVEN!

had one? Try Brad Pitt, Christian Slater, Lenny Kravitz, Rod Stewart, Julian Lennon, The Edge, John F. Kennedy, Jr., Ashley Hamilton (that's Mr. Shannen Doherty to you), and Bruce Willis.

February 1994 Ethan Hawk's character in the *Über*-twenty something movie *Reality Bites* is accused by Winona Ryder's character of turning her living room "into a den of slack." His character sports a goatee, reads *Being and Time* in luncheonettes, sings in a band, and won't get a real job.

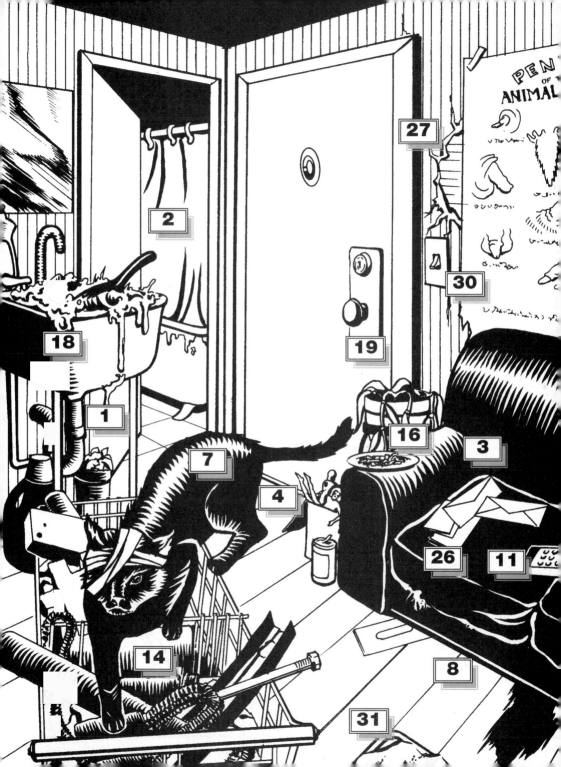

FIRST-TIME VISITORS TO YOUR HOME SHOULD RESPOND TO IT THE WAY URBAN SOPHISTICATES DID WHEN CONFRONTED WITH THE TRANSGRESSIVE PERFORMANCE ART OF THE EARLY SEVENTIES: THOUGH INWARDLY SHOCKED AND DISGUSTED, THEY MUST ALWAYS ACT UNFAZED AND POLITE.

EVOKING SUCH A VISCERAL RESPONSE WITHOUT THE HELP OF A HIGHLY PAID DOMESTIC DESIGN PROFESSIONAL IS NOT EASY. IT TAKES A KEEN EYE TO PULL TOGETHER WILDLY DISPARATE DESIGN ELEMENTS—PARTICULARLY THOSE DESIGN ELEMENTS SHOPLIFTED WITHOUT SO MUCH AS A FLEETING THOUGHT GIVEN TO THE ROOM'S DOMINANT COLOR SCHEME—AND CREATE AN INSPIRED "WHOLE."

YOU'LL KNOW YOU'VE ACHIEVED THE DESIRED EFFECT WHEN YOU ARE STRUCK BY AN INEXPLICABLE FRISSON EACH TIME YOU OPEN THE FRONT DOOR. (UNFORTUNATELY, SOME PEOPLE HAVE BEEN KNOWN TO CONFUSE THIS WITH THE WALL OF SCENT EMANATING FROM THE CAT BOX. YOU DO SO AT YOUR OWN PERIL.)

1. Dead creeping charlie
2. Joe Cool shower curtain bought with Camel Cash
3. Threatening, abusive letters from bill collectors
4. Collection of violently defaced Barbie dolls
5. Cans of tuna stolen from friends' houses
6. African fertility figurine
7. Cat, tragically maimed in freak electrical accident
8. Hole in floor
9. Stuffed armadillo
10. Dirty socks
11. Remote control
12. Batik bed sheet covering mysterious brown stain on wall
13. Important scraps of paper
14. Shop-Rite shopping cart filled with materials scavenged from nearby construction site for newest art project
15. Overflowing ashtray
16. Heap of smokable butts
17. Stack of unpaid phone bills
18. Sink filled with Class 6 hazardous materials (HazMat suit required for anyone approaching within a five-foot radius)
19. Dead Wandering Jew
20. Deck of nudie girl cards
21. Twinkly Christmas lights
22. Space heater
23. Mural commemorating the 1984 McDonald's massacre in San Ysidro, California, done in the style of Picasso's Guernica (gift from ex-girlfriend)
24. Pile of unread newspapers
25. Mandolin
26. Crab colony living on sofa cushions (Legacy of likable drifter who squatted your living room for two months)
27. Head-butt hole in wall (Legacy of likable drifter who squatted your living room for two months)
28. Futon
29. Bed sheets sporting Shroud of Turin-like imprint of sleeping body
30. "Penises of the Animal Kingdom" poster
31. Overflowing cat box
32. Marijuana seeds
33. Dying ficus
34. Stash of pornographic magazines

INSIDE THE BOTTOM DRESSER DRAWER
1. Dusty condom
2. Embarrassing high school picture
3. Baseball card collection currently on the block
4. Emergency provisions hidden from housemates
5. Frank Frazzetta book
6. Mothballs hidden by mother

Laundry: Mirror of the Self

Laundry: Mirror of the Self

LAUNDRY SITUATION	PSYCHIC STATE
Heaped in four-foot mound on closet floor	TORMENTED BY PANGS OF MORTALITY
Strewn artfully about the room	ALIENATED FROM THE SELF
Mildewing within stolen plastic clothes basket	GRIPPED BY UNEXPRESSED RAGE
Scrunched in bottom of oblong duffel bag	CAUGHT IN THE THROES OF MORTAL DESPAIR
Dangling from hooks/draped over chairs/hanging from doorknob	HAUNTED BY JUNGIAN SHADOW SELF
Jammed under the bed	AFFLICTED WITH APOCALYPTIC VISIONS
Resting inside dormant clothes dryer	PRACTICING AVOIDANCE
Stolen from laundromat by mysterious roaming sociopath	OVERCOME BY MANIC PARANOIA
Folded neatly in dresser drawers	TRAGICALLY, IRREVERSIBLY MENTALLY ILL

HOW to Forestall the Inevitable: UTILITY TERMINATION AND YOU

The phone bill has arrived in the yellow envelope. Again.

THE ELECTRIC BILL IS IN THE DREADED PINK ENVELOPE. DITTO, THE GAS BILL.
Come to think of it, every time you open your mailbox a new utility bill has materialized, sheathed in an attention-grabbing pastel envelope.

There's not a whole lot you can do about those pesky credit card people who leave messages on your answering machine and insist on bugging you while you're at work ("Could you please call Tom Gardener at 1-800-555-3746, extension 211 at your earliest convenience." Sure you'll call. *Right away*.) They're going to cut off your credit card capabilities pretty much no matter what you tell them.

But while having a credit card turned off is a minor inconvenience, having your telephone, electricity, or gas turned off can be an unmitigated bummer. Before you resign yourself to taking cold showers and running to the U-Totem for phone calls, be proactive—get out of bed and give *them* a call.

PLAN A: Sick Baby

Claim that you have a SICK BABY in the house and therefore you need EMERGENCY UTILITY SERVICE for at least the next THREE WEEKS.

PLAN B: DEAD HOUSEMATE

Claim that you have a DEAD HOUSEMATE who unfortunately recently suffered a DEATH that was both TRAGIC and UNTIMELY. Admit to being OVERWROUGHT WITH GRIEF and respectfully request EMERGENCY UTILITY SERVICE for A FEW WEEKS until his finances can be put into order.

PLAN D: ASTHMA SUFFERER

Claim that you are an ASTHMA SUFFERER and that the TELEPHONE is your LIFELINE, and if they turn it off you might not be able to get EMERGENCY MEDICAL HELP when you need it. If the ELECTRICITY goes you might not be able to locate your INHALER in a moment of PANIC. If they decide to turn off the HEAT, well, they might as well just pour MAPLE SYRUP down your WINDPIPE. Do they really want to KILL YOU for a lousy sixty bucks?

PLAN C: Crime Scene

Claim that your DEAD HOUSEMATE met his VIOLENT DEMISE in THIS VERY HOUSE! It is thus a bona fide CRIME SCENE and you would most respectfully request EMERGENCY UTILITY SERVICE for the next SEVERAL WEEKS so the POLICE can proceed with their investigation.

PLAN E: Quarantine

Claim that your house has been QUARANTINED by the regional head of HEALTH AND HUMAN SERVICES due to an unfortunate outbreak of CHOLERA which had been FESTERING IN THE BOWELS of your buddy Darin who is just back from his WHIRLWIND TOUR OF SOUTH AMERICA. You most respectfully request EMERGENCY UTILITY SERVICE for the next MONTH OR SO, or until the quarantine is lifted, whichever comes first.

ODE TO THE FUTON

I met a girl, she had clean sheets;
I lived with her for several weeks.
She kicked me out, heels over head;
A carpet scrap was then my bed.
I did my time on floor, on couch,
I sofa surfed, arose a grouch.
And then one day I came upon
that curbside coup, a used futon!

Serta Perfect Sleeper,
Sealy Posturepedic,
Sterns and Foster, Springmade—
Hell I just don't need it.

Brownish with age, wine-stained,
and smelly
(I *hope* that that weird blot was jelly).
I dueled to the death with an odd creeping
mildew.
'Twas not a nice sight; believe what I tell you.
Butt-charred and troughed, thin as a rag,
Just like an econo-sized Kotex mini pad.

Serta Perfect Sleeper,
Sealy Posturepedic,
Sterns and Foster, Springmade—
their purpose I don't see it.

I won't dial toll-free MATTRES,
I won't shell out the bucks.
I'll stick with my free futon—
I don't care if it sucks.
It's more than just a bed now;
It's cat box, couch, and more—
It's hardened foam,
My house and home,
For countless hours a-slept on.

When Your House Is, **Uh,** Your Home:

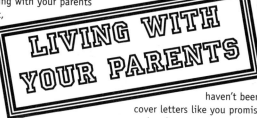

While it's true that living with your parents smacks of the pathetic, sometimes you just have to suck it up for a while and avail yourself of the amenities of home. No one needs to tell you that your feeble attempts to put a roof over your head will never amount to what can be had, virtually for free, within your parents' home. Dishwasher. Garbage disposal. Non-coin-operated washer and dryer. *Ice maker.*

That said, moving in with your parents should always be regarded as a short-term solution for what will essentially be a lifelong problem. There's nothing wrong with a little temporary economic asylum, but you don't want to turn into a thirty-year-old failed novelist working on a spec script for *Saved by the Bell* while your aging parents cheer you on.

If you do end up back at home for a while, it can help to think of the situation as simply "squatting your old bedroom": living on, rent free, while doing your best to avert local hostilities and avoid getting thrown out on the street. You'll spend a few relaxing months unearthing old *Star Wars* figurines from boxes in the basement and scanning the sex ads in the local free newspaper. When your parents realize you haven't been polishing up those cover letters like you promised, they'll wise up and make you start paying rent.

In order to make a long-term go of it at home, you must be entangled in just the right web of family dysfunction, where, say, your codependent mother, desperate to avoid spending her golden years cooped up with your boozing, emotionally unavailable father, makes your bed and irons your underwear and hands you money in order to make you stay on. But be forewarned: Even in this best case scenario you might be forced, periodically, to do some yard work. For the rest of us—those who weren't blessed when God was doling out toxic nuclear families—residing at home can quickly come dangerously close to a living hell. When this happens, you have but one option: find an eighteen-hour-a-week job and a $175-a-month room in a house spilling over with like-minded slackers.

(Try to steal some furniture on your way out.)

THE COOL PARENT EQUATION

Unfortunately it's not always clear whether or not it will be to your advantage to move in with your parents. The Cool Parent Equation was designed to help you in your decision making, to take you beyond a crass financial analysis and into the realm of important quality-of-life intangibles. Calibrate your estimates on the basis of a typical month in your parents' house (astronomical measurements should be in kilometers).

$$(\text{cash handouts}) - 2\left[\text{hours worth of chores/yard work} + \pi(\text{\# of harangues about getting a job})\right]$$

$$+$$

$$\frac{1}{2}\left[\frac{\text{dollar value of free long-distance call}}{\text{\# of complaints when you stay out all night}}\right]$$

$$+$$

$$\frac{1}{3}\left[\frac{\text{\# of times you get to use their car}}{\text{\# of times they wake you up early}}\right]$$

$$-\left[(\text{rent they make you pay})(\text{approximate distance between the earth and the sun})\right]$$

$$= X$$

If **X > 0**, go ahead and live at home
If **X < 0**, get yourself an apartment

The ABCs of Squatting

SQUATTING IS A RATHER EXTREME SOLUTION TO THE RENT PROBLEM, AND ONE THAT IS USUALLY MORE TROUBLE THAN IT'S WORTH. PASSING OUT FLIERS ON STREET CORNERS FOR RENT MONEY IS MUCH EASIER THAN, SAY, REHABILITING ABANDONED BUILDINGS WITH JUNK SCAVENGED FROM CONSTRUCTION SITES AND DIVING INTO KENTUCKY FRIED CHICKEN DUMPSTERS FOR YOUR SUPPER EACH NIGHT. IF YOU END UP SQUATTING FOR MORE THAN A COUPLE OF MONTHS YOU'LL BEGIN TO RESEMBLE YOUR ACQUAINTANCES IN THE LUNATIC FRINGE, TAKING THOSE TEENAGE ANARCHIST LEANINGS A BIT TOO SERIOUSLY AND SURRENDERING INTIMATE TERRAIN IN YOUR LOSING BATTLE WITH SCABIES AND BODY LICE.

THAT SAID, AND WITH THE FURTHER DISCLAIMER THAT SQUATTING IS STILL ILLEGAL IN THE UNITED STATES AND THE FOLLOWING IS INTENDED FOR INFORMATIONAL PURPOSES ONLY, THIS IS MORE OR LESS HOW YOU DO IT:

FIND A BUILDING: Look for a building that is clearly abandoned—totally boarded up, with no real estate sign out front—yet looks like it could be made "livable." Check out the inside and then take some time to feel out the neighbors. Do your best to convince them that you're responsible, if not exactly law-abiding, citizens and that it would be to their advantage to have you inside that house instead of a passel of crack-head degenerates.

CHECK OUT THE TAX SITUATION: TAKE THE ADDRESS TO THE TAX RECORD OFFICE TO FIND OUT ITS CURRENT STATUS. IF IT'S OWNED BY THE GOVERNMENT OR THERE ARE MORE THAN $1,000 OF BACK TAXES OWED ON THE PROPERTY, IT'S PROBABLY A GOOD PROSPECT.

MOVE IN AND FIX IT UP: You'll want to squat with a group of like-minded people, because it makes it safer *and* you have more hands to help with the physical labor. First you should secure the building with good locks, clean it up, and do some basic weatherproofing. Then figure out a way to scam some utility hookups, belly up to the soup kitchen door, and panhandle for drug and alcohol research.

DUMPSTER DIVING

DUMPSTER DIVING INVOLVES CLIMBING INTO A GARBAGE DUMPSTER AND SCROUNGING AROUND INSIDE IT FOR THINGS YOU CAN EITHER USE YOURSELF OR RESELL. WEAR STURDY BOOTS AND YOUR WORST CLOTHES, AND BRING A LONG STICK WITH WHICH TO POKE ANYTHING THAT LOOKS LIKE IT MIGHT HAVE ONCE BEEN ATTACHED TO A HUMAN BODY.

TRASH PICKING IS LOW-IMPACT DUMPSTER DIVING, LIMITED TO CITIES AND TOWNS IN WHICH BAGS OF GARBAGE ARE PROPPED AGAINST THE CURB ON TRASH DAY. THE TRASH PICKER FORAGES FOR DISTINCTIVE CURBSIDE ACQUISITIONS WHILE WALKING TO AND FROM HIS HOME, STOPPING TO PEEK INSIDE A PROMISING BAG WHILE GOING ABOUT HIS ORDINARY BUSINESS. (IN THE RIGHT NEIGHBORHOOD, A CHARRED POTHOLDER WON'T LAST ON A CURB FOR MORE THAN FIFTEEN MINUTES.)

FREE FOOD IN THE MAIL

"HELLO, JIFFY? YES, WELL, I JUST WANTED TO SAY THAT MY HUSBAND AND I ARE LONGTIME USERS OF YOUR PRODUCT . . . YOU'RE WELCOME, YEAH, WE'VE BEEN USING IT FOR A LONG TIME, AND WE LIKE THE SMOOTH KIND BECAUSE WE HAVE A SMALL CHILD AND WE'RE VERY SENSITIVE ABOUT THINGS LIKE THAT . . . WELL, I OPENED UP THE PEANUT BUTTER AND ABOUT HALFWAY DOWN THERE WAS THIS BLACK THING, THIS LITTLE HARD BLACK THING . . . MAYBE IT WAS A BURNED PEANUT, I COULDN'T TELL, I THREW THE WHOLE THING AWAY . . . NO, I KNOW IT DIDN'T COME FROM ANYWHERE IN MY HOUSEHOLD, I'M A GOOD HOUSEKEEPER, BELIEVE ME, IT WAS IN YOUR PEANUT BUTTER . . . OF COURSE, WELL, THANK YOU VERY MUCH, YOU'VE BEEN VERY KIND, AND LIKE I SAID, WE'RE LIFELONG CUSTOMERS . . . HI, PREGO? YEAH, I JUST THOUGHT YOU OUGHT TO KNOW THAT I FOUND SOMETHING REALLY GROSS LAST NIGHT IN A JAR OF YOUR MEAT SAUCE. . . ."

DO FERRETS STINK? HOUSE PETS AS SURROGATE CHILDREN

THERE WILL COME A TIME IN YOUR LIFE WHEN YOU WILL HAVE TO FIND A SATISFACTORY ANSWER TO THE ENDURING QUESTION: "IF I MOVE TO PRAGUE, WHO'S GOING TO TAKE CARE OF MY CAT?" INDEED, ASSUMING LONG-TERM CUSTODY OF A HOUSE PET IS A DECISION THAT SHOULD NOT BE MADE HASTILY. PROBABLY THE CLOSEST YOU'LL EVER GET TO BONA FIDE RESPONSIBILITY. AS SUCH, IT FOR SOME OF YOUR PEERS, THE PET-OWNING IMPULSE IS NOT UNLIKE THE FORCE THAT COMPELS THIRTEEN-YEAR-OLD GIRLS TO KEEP THEIR BABIES—THEY WANT TO HAVE SOMETHING TO CARE FOR AND TO LOVE. FOR OTHERS, THE PET-OWNING IMPULSE IS AKIN TO THE FORCE THAT COMPELS THIRTEEN-YEAR-OLD GIRLS TO CONCEIVE THOSE BABIES—IT SEEMS LIKE A GOOD IDEA AT THE TIME. EITHER WAY, THE PET MUST BE FED, WATCHED OVER, AND KEPT HEALTHY, OFTEN AT CONSIDERABLE COST. (ODDLY ENOUGH, MOST SLACK PETS HAVE SOME SORT OF DISABILITY, BE IT MENTAL OR PHYSICAL, THAT WOULD CAUSE AN INDIVIDUAL WITH MORE "TRADITIONAL" AMERICAN VALUES TO BREEZE RIGHT PAST IT AT THE POUND AND PERMIT IT TO BE EUTHANIZED WITHOUT A SECOND THOUGHT. FOR INSTANCE, THREE-LEGGED DOGS ARE CURRENTLY IN VOGUE, BUT MENTALLY RETARDED CATS, ONE-EYED FERRETS, AND EMOTIONALLY CHALLENGED GOLDFISH ARE ALSO POPULAR SLACK PETS. THE BURNING QUESTION—UH, DID YOUR CAT COME WITHOUT THAT LEG?—IS, QUITE OFTEN, A DIFFICULT ONE TO ASK.)

HOW TO MAKE
HALLUCINOGENIC
DRUGS
FROM SIMPLE HOUSEHOLD
CHEMICALS

Ha! Just kidding.

TOP 10 CITIES TO SLACK IN

WHAT IS IT THAT MAKES ONE TOWN A VERITABLE HOTBED OF SLACKERS WHILE A NEIGHBORING BURGH IS HOME INSTEAD TO COUNTLESS RESPONSIBLE TAX-PAYING CITIZENS? DUMB LUCK?

Perhaps. But there are a few definable factors that make a city hospitable to the urban nomad, namely: pockets boasting affordable rents, a vibrant local art and music scene, and a service-industry economy anxious to chew up tender young college graduates. Midwestern cities that boast both the state capitol and a state university are prime slack locales, as the convergence of conservative politics and liberal academics often results in freaks spewing forth from the woodwork. And then of course there are the intangibles: an atmosphere of tolerance higher than the regional average, a thriving alternative culture, and a reputation as a painless place to live.

1. **Austin, Texas**
2. **Boston, Massachusetts**
3. **Chapel Hill, North Carolina**
4. **Lawrence, Kansas**
5. **Madison, Wisconsin**
6. **Philadelphia, Pennsylvania**
7. **Portland, Oregon**
8. **Providence, Rhode Island**
9. **San Francisco, California**
10. **Tempe, Arizona**

The Unwritten Rules: Mastering Cafe Etiquette

A cafe is not a coffee shop. Nor is it a diner. It's neither a sandwich place nor a quaint cappuccino-brewing patisserie where suburban ladies go to drink low-fat lattes and gab. It is actually a cross between a neighborhood bar and your very own living room, minus the eau de beer and the undergarments strewn artfully across the sofa.

Every cafe is governed by a set of inviolable rules known only to the initiated, not unlike those familiar to frequent visitors to your own home (Use the brown sock as a coaster; Don't mention the smell). If you elect to hang out in a cafe yet choose to overlook any of the following rules, be advised that you do so at your peril:

DO-Tip the counterpeople, no matter how slow, rude, and/or obnoxious they happen to be.

DON'T-Wait for them to absent-mindedly shake the "Tips Are Much Appreciated" jar under your nose while you are fumbling with the zipper on your tiny Peruvian change purse.

DO-Feel free to eavesdrop on the conversations at neighboring tables.

DON'T-Talk loudly about how this place used to be cool until it was over-run with posers and idiots.

DO-Pet the dog.

DON'T-Regale your fellow cafe-goers with a list of the health regula-tions that are violated by the dog's habit of sniffing the produce.

DO-Go ahead and brew a new pot of coffee if the supply is low.

DON'T-Ask for decaf.

DO-Read their newspaper in order to save money.

DON'T-Fill in the crossword puzzle without express written permission from the staff.

DO-Strike up a conversation with the antisocial loner methodically burning pages of his poetry in an ashtray at the table by the window.

DON'T-Let him follow you home.

13 Weighty Questions to Ponder While Sitting in a Cafe

1. IS THERE A GOD?
2. DO I EXIST?
3. IF SO, HOW COME?
4. WHAT IF I'M REALLY JUST A MINOR CHARACTER IN THAT CREEPY GUY OVER THERE'S DREAM?
5. THAT WOULD MEAN I COULD STOP WORRYING ABOUT PAYING MY RENT, RIGHT?
6. WHAT IS THE NATURE OF EVIL?
7. WHAT DO YOU SUPPOSE IS THE HALF-LIFE OF THIS HICKEY?
8. AM I BEING PARANOID, OR IS MR. CREEPY GUY LOOKING AT ME?
9. IS THAT WOMAN BEHIND THE COUNTER WEARING A BRA?
10. SHOULD I GO AHEAD AND PIERCE MY GENITALS?
11. WAS THELMA REALLY A LESBIAN?
12. WHAT IF E DOESN'T EQUAL MC SQUARED?
13. IS THIS THE SAME CHEESECAKE THEY WERE SERVING YESTERDAY?

THE CAFE-GOER'S WHO'S WHO

2

1

4

3

5

3. THE GIRL WHO SITS FOR HOURS FLIPPING THROUGH OLD *NEW YORKER*S AND LOOKING BORED: Williams grad. Smokes thin brown cigarettes. Can't help but favorably compare her collection of unpublished stories to those she finds in the Magazine Of Record. Keeps a fabric-covered blank book filled with pithy observations tucked in her many-colored Guatemalan tote bag. Of course, she would never refer to it as a *tote bag* ("how hopelessly *suburban*").

4. THE ETCHER: Proud owner of a small, spiral-bound notebook filled with pen-and-ink drawings on acid-free paper. Asks attractive cafe-goers if he can attempt to sketch their likeness. Often seen handing out his business card to newfound friends ("artist/philosopher/caterer").

5. THE DOG: Wears a bandanna around his neck and smiles a lot. Whose dog is it? Who knows? Who cares? He's the communal dog, and we know that because he licks the boneless free-range chicken breasts while they're sitting on the counter and no one sees fit to complain.

1. THE NIHILIST: Wears a standard-issue black turtleneck, even in the dead of summer. Occasionally retires to the rest room for a lengthy visit, undoubtedly overcome by debilitating existential angst or the need for mind-altering drugs.

2. THE AGING HIPPIE: Balding. Views the burgeoning cafe scene as an ideal way to pick up nubile young babes. Everyone secretly worries that they might wake up twenty years from now and *be* him.

6. THE POETESS: Long straight hair and glasses. Remains hopelessly in the grip of the Sylvia Plath complex that the rest of us outgrew in junior high. Gives vent to her neuroses in thoughtful, complex poems that she crafts in public because doing so makes her feel less alienated from the world at large.

7. THE WEASLY LITTLE GUY WHO'S ALWAYS TRYING TO BUM A CIGARETTE: Gets on everyone's already overtaxed nerves.

8. THE CONSPIRACY THEORIST: Sports a dingy white undershirt and fatigues cut off at the knee. Tries to initiate conversations with other cafe-goers about JFK and UFOs. Their disinterest adds to his escalating feeling of alienation.

THE PERFORMANCE ARTIST: Asks people at neighboring tables if he can videotape them having sex.

THE FREELANCE GENIUS: Ruminates a lot, and complains about the coffee.

THE CREATIVE-LOOKING GUY WHOSE EXACT TALENT IS HARD TO PIN DOWN, EVEN FOR HIM: Busboy by night, singularly morose artist by day. Twentysomething, with long dark hair and an odd, sparse goatee. Feels an overwhelming need to express himself but hasn't figured out just quite *how*.

THE GUY READING *ZEN AND THE ART OF MOTORCYCLE MAINTENANCE.* The cafe neophyte. Everyone stops at his table to tell him how good the book is, how it changed their lives, helped them make *connections*.

THE WRITER: Stares out the window at parked cars for inspiration, then hunches over her table and scribbles furiously. Stares out the window at the parked cars

some more. Gets up to refill her coffee cup. Hurries back to her table and scribbles some more. Everyone else is tres intrigued.

THE MUSICIAN: Currently in search of a band. Spends time in the cafe scanning want ads and putting up fliers printed on pieces of paper that span the commercially available day-glo spectrum.

THE GUY WHO LIVES IN HIS VOLKSWAGEN BUG WITH THIRTEEN MANGY DOGS: Reeks, even after giving himself a spit bath in the cafe's powder room. Nurses a single cup of coffee for hours.

THE TWO LADY SHOPPERS WHO WANDERED IN, ACCIDENTALLY: They chat. They chat loudly about things like clothing labels and vacation spots, oblivious to the hate beams emanating from the eyes of the neo-Marxist contingent assembling pita sandwiches behind the counter. Their thoughts, after scanning the crowd, can be summed up by the sentence "Do your mothers know you dress like this?"

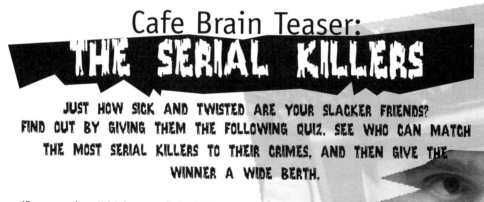

Cafe Brain Teaser:
THE SERIAL KILLERS

JUST HOW SICK AND TWISTED ARE YOUR SLACKER FRIENDS? FIND OUT BY GIVING THEM THE FOLLOWING QUIZ. SEE WHO CAN MATCH THE MOST SERIAL KILLERS TO THEIR CRIMES, AND THEN GIVE THE WINNER A WIDE BERTH.

(Bonus point: Which one of the killers is actually, technically, a mass murderer?)

THE KILLERS:

1. Genene Jones
2. Albert DeSalvo
3. Richard Biegenwald
4. Aileen Wuornos
5. Jeffrey Dahmer
6. Carlton Gary
7. Coral Watts

8. Gary Heidnik
9. Edward Gein
10. Charles Manson
11. Dennis Nilsen
12. Ted Bundy
13. John Wayne Gacy
14. Richard Speck

15. Henry Lee Lucas
16. Arthur Shawcross
17. Wayne B. Williams
18. Kenneth Bianchi
19. Edmund J. Cody
20. David Berkowitz

☐ Convicted of killing his ninth wife, Letha Gay, after her remains were found decomposing in the trunk of his car. Suspected of killing at least another four of his wives, while the remaining four are officially listed as "missing."

☐ The "Sunday Morning Slasher"; confessed to killing more than forty black women in Houston with a large knife.

☐ The "Stocking Strangler"; killed nine prominent elderly women in their homes in Columbus, Georgia.

☐ Infamous Milwaukee homosexual cannibal; confessed to seventeen murders.

☐ Thought to be responsible for the Atlanta Child Murders. Convicted of killing one victim on circumstantial evidence, but some people think the real killer is still at large.

☐ English homosexual necrophiliac; reported to have remarked that the weight of a severed head, when picked up by the hair, is far greater than one would imagine.

☐ "Son of Sam"; terrorized New York City and corresponded in print with *New York Daily News* columnist Jimmy Breslin.

☐ Abducted, raped, chained, impregnated, and sometimes killed and cannibalized women in the basement of his Philadelphia home.

☐ "Upstanding" citizen who picked up young boys at bus stations, only to torture and murder them and bury the bodies in the basement of his suburban Chicago home. Crime was reported by his wife who complained of odors coming from under the house.

☐ "The Genesee River Killer"; strangled, butchered, and cannibalized eleven women. Was caught by police when seen casually eating his lunch while the nude corpse of his latest victim floated past him on the Genesee river.

☐ Convicted of murdering two women in a Florida college dorm and a twelve-year-old girl. Also linked to countless murders in Seattle and Salt Lake City, he was apparently upset with his fiancé for breaking up with him.

☐ The "Boston Strangler"; gained entrance to apartments by masquerading as a handyman, then strangled his victims.

☐ Stalked attractive high school cheerleaders in New Jersey; buried their remains in the backyard of his mother's Staten Island home.

☐ Convicted of only one, but suspected in the murders of sixty-one other babies at the Bexar County Administrative Medical Center in San Antonio.

☐ Warned parole board he would kill again when released from the Michigan State Penn for killing his mother, then killed a woman shortly after his release and dumped her body within walking distance of the prison gate.

☐ Inaccurately touted as the first female serial killer; confessed to killing seven men in Florida but claimed they were all done in self-defense.

☐ Head of "family" of California killers; claimed to have killed thirty-five people.

☐ Backwoods cannibalistic killer who terrorized Plainfield, Wisconsin; the inspiration for the Norman Bates character in the movie *Psycho*.

☐ Brutally slayed eight student nurses in Chicago.

☐ The "Hillside Strangler"; was convicted of killing nine young women in L.A. with the help of his sidekick, Angelo Buono, Jr.

ANSWERS:

Bonus: Richard Speck

1n; 2l; 3m; 4p; 5d; 6c; 7b; 8h; 9r; 10q; 11f; 12k; 13i; 14s; 15o; 16j; 17e; 18t; 19a; 20g

WHY WE SMOKE CIGARETTES

- Pithy Surgeon General warnings on packs a handy reminder of our own mortality

- Nicotine generates a relatively cost-efficient buzz

- Gives us something to fiddle with while we're busy thinking

- Noxious secondhand smoke miraculously repels self-righteous Boomer ex-smokers we encounter in public places

- Daily brush with death can be invigorating

ALCOHOLISM ON A SHOESTRING BUDGET

LIQUOR CORDIALS: TURN GRANDMA'S CANDY BOWL INTO A TASTY HAPPY HOUR.

TABLE SCORE: Any glass without a butt is fair game.

THE FORTY: COST-CONSCIOUS CONSUMERS ALWAYS CHECK THE LABEL FOR THE WORDS "MALT" OR "MALTED."

BAR SLUDGE: Your friend the bartender might make you a drink out of the tasty alcoholic blend festering in the bottom of the speed rack.

ROBO-DOSE: REMEMBER, AN OPEN MEDICINE CABINET IS AN OPEN BAR.

Hemp vs. Coke: A Drug Primer

HEMP	COKE
Cheap	-EXPENSIVE
Possession = misdemeanor in most states	-POSSESSION = FELONY IN MOST STATES
Chemical form of complacency	-CHEMICAL FORM OF AMBITION
Suited to the lazy, do-nothing lifestyle of the laid-back slacker	-SUITED TO THE INTENSE, FAST-PACED LIFESTYLE OF THE RAPACIOUS YOUNG PROFESSIONAL
Dealer is your friend/roommate/brother	-DEALER WILL MAIM YOU FOR NONPAYMENT
Food tastes great	-YOU STOP EATING
Music sounds great	-MUSIC IS DROWNED OUT BY THE SOUND OF YOUR OWN DRONING VOICE
You have interesting thoughts about what it would be like to meet Aristotle	-YOU BECOME CONVINCED THAT YOU ARE THE MOST INTELLIGENT, CREATIVE, POWERFUL PERSON OF THIS CENTURY
Someone steals your pot? Get pissed off and ask him if he wouldn't like to borrow your pipe as well	-SOMEONE STEALS YOUR COKE? TIE HIM TO THE GROUND AND SLOWLY PEEL OFF HIS SKIN WITH A RUG CUTTER
10 A.M. the next day: Wake up feeling puzzled and mildly disoriented	-10 A.M. THE NEXT DAY: AT COKE DEALER'S DOOR AFTER PAWNING ROOMMATE'S STEREO FOR A HUNDRED BUCKS
Long-term use makes you stupid	-LONG-TERM USE MAKES YOU DIE

The Chess-Playing Slacker

ONE OF THE EASIEST WAYS TO VAULT YOURSELF UP INTO THE RANKS OF THE SLACK ELITE IS TO TAKE UP THE GAME OF CHESS. THE MERE ACT OF SITTING DOWN IN FRONT OF A CHESSBOARD WITH A LOOK OF SEVERE CONCENTRATION PASTED ON YOUR FACE IS ENOUGH TO GARNER INTELLECTUAL RESPECT IN SOME SLACK CIRCLES. IN OTHERS, UNFORTUNATELY, YOUR REPUTATION WILL ALSO DEPEND ON HOW WELL YOU PLAY. IDEALLY YOU'LL STUMBLE UPON A CAFE WHOSE SLACK DENIZENS ARE ALL TOO BUSY TO PLAY CHESS, PREFERRING TO DOODLE IN THEIR NOTEBOOKS AND STARE MEANINGFULLY OUT INTO SPACE INSTEAD. IF YOU ARE PERSISTENT IN SETTING UP THE BOARD AND PESTERING PEOPLE TO PLAY WITH YOU EACH DAY, YOUR STOCK WILL RISE DRAMATICALLY EVEN IF YOU NEVER UTTER A SINGLE "CHECKMATE."

Darts

Bowling

Skee-ball

Pool

Pinball

Masturbation

Skateboarding

Backgammon

Poker

Scrabble

Pinochle

Checkers

Crossword puzzles

Rolling bums

Kickball

Surfing

Skiing

T'ai chi

Bacchanalian orgies

Gin rummy

Chess

Video games

Fooz-ball

Celebrity stalking

Golf

Duck hunting

Skeet shooting

Squash

Fencing

Croquet

Shuffleboard

Jogging

Yoga

Archery

Tackle football

Lawn bowling

Ice fishing

Word jumbles

Smear the queer

Cliff diving

Body building

Big game
hunting

Seven minutes
in heaven

Stamp collecting

Arm wrestling

Yachting

MY HOBBIES

-PICKING UP THINGS OFF THE GROUND

   -SITTING ON MY STEPS AND WATCHING THINGS

-DRINKING JUG WINE UNTIL UNCONSCIOUS

      -LISTENING TO PEOPLE TALK FOR HOURS UPON END IN
          SMALL ROOMS WHILE UNDER THE INFLUENCE OF
-CALLING 1-800 NUMBERS   CAFFEINE AND NICOTINE

      -CREATING IMAGINARY WORLDS THAT EXIST ONLY IN MY MIND

            -STARTING FIRES

                  -SLEEPING

WANDERLUST

PRETEND FOR A MOMENT THAT YOU'RE A COLLEGE GRADUATE WHO HAS BEEN MANNING THE REGISTER AT A LIQUOR STORE IN ANN ARBOR FOR THE PAST THREE YEARS. IMAGINE THAT YOU'RE THE SORT OF PERSON WHO OCCASIONALLY CRAFTS INSULTING LITTLE NOTES ADDRESSED TO HUMANITY IN GENERAL AND STICKS THEM TO THE STORE'S SWINGING GLASS DOOR. YOU LIKE JOY DIVISION. YOU FREQUENTLY WEAR SKI CAPS INDOORS.

Now, pretend you're a college graduate who has been manning the register at a liquor store in Ann Arbor for the past three years, but one who—while still enjoying obnoxious little notes, Joy Division, and functional thermal outerwear—also happens to be making plans to go *someplace else*.

Chronic wanderlust is the ultimate psychic refuge of the responsibility-averse slacker. Once your vague dissatisfaction with life has time to crystallize around your slack surroundings—the skeezy smell in your refrigerator, the way your housemate breathes—you'll begin to plan your escape.

The fact that you've *already* escaped the bulk of responsibilities and headaches that accompany normal life ought not alarm you. *Normal life* is what's alarming. Normal life, when you stop to think about it, is utterly appalling.

It's an unfortunate fact of life that most of your fantasy travel plans will have to hinge on the tragic, untimely deaths of one or more members of your immediate family. These deaths must be mercifully quick and call for an absolute minimum of hospitalization and expensive nursing home care. In lieu of this, you will be forced to save up some money on your own.

But don't let that sobering note stop you from dreaming. Whether or not a given journey ever actually, technically occurs is not nearly as important as the amount of planning that goes into it. Exotic travel shows viewed on cable, phone calls made to bucket shop plane ticket vendors, drug-trafficking horror stories recounted by strangers you meet at cafes—these are the important things.

You might consider Europe. If you do it right, you can swing two, maybe three years of avoiding reality with a bunch of Australians, busking in the Paris Metro and scrubbing youth hostel toilets for free room and board. It goes without saying that you would be able to write much better poems if you could write them while watching the sun slip behind a crumbling Doric temple. But, face it, if you schlepp a backpack and three pairs of mildewy underwear around long enough, anything starts to look good. You'll come back and settle down, quite willingly, to a life of hard-core reality. When you wake up in a sweat in the middle of the night, after dreaming about parking tickets or bridgework, you'll say to yourself, "At least I have a drawerful of pristine undergarments. Perhaps I'll even purchase some more."

YOU COULD BE EXOTIC AND GO TO JAPAN, BUT YOU WOULDN'T REALLY BE THAT EXOTIC BECAUSE JUST ABOUT EVERYBODY IS GOING TO JAPAN THESE DAYS SO NOBODY WILL BE TOO IMPRESSED, REALLY. RUMOR HAS IT YOU CAN EARN $50 AN HOUR TEACHING ENGLISH, WHICH SHOULD JUST ABOUT COVER THE RENT OF YOUR CLIMATE-CONTROLLED SLUMBER TUBE. AND YOU'LL HAVE TO EAT RAW FISH EYES, OCCASIONALLY, IF YOU DON'T WANT TO OFFEND YOUR HOSTS.

YOUR BEST OPTION, CLEARLY, IS TO SET OFF IN SEARCH OF THE MYTHICAL AMERICAN LANDSCAPE ON A GREYHOUND BUS AND TRY TO WRITE A BOOK ABOUT THE EXPERIENCE. WHILE THAT *PARTICULAR* BOOK HAS ALREADY BEEN WRITTEN, WHO SAYS YOU COULDN'T WRITE A BOOK ABOUT ONE OF THE FOLLOWING:

1. Setting off in search of the mythical American landscape by riding around on a Greyhound bus and eating at old-time diners in small towns with weird names.

2. Setting off in search of the mythical American landscape by riding around on a Greyhound bus and striking up conversations with colorful old people who live in small towns with weird names and hang out in old-time diners.

3. Setting off in search of the mythical American landscape by riding around on a Greyhound bus and having sex with your fellow passengers.

SLACKER PILGRIMAGES

AUSTIN

Austin, Texas. Ground zero of the slack *zeitgeist*. And, not coincidentally, the setting of Richard Linklater's ground-breaking work, the film that gave Those You Dare Not Give A Name a name. Journeying to Austin after your eleventh or twelfth viewing of *Slacker* is sort of like walking through Salzburg after watching *The Sound of Music*. (Although you would never watch *The Sound of Music* except, perhaps, at gunpoint, so the analogy only goes so far.) Anyhow, go ahead and peddle your plasma at Pharma-co, hit Les Amis and Quackenbush's, and walk in the footsteps of the *Slacker* slackers: the Pap Smear Pusher, the Dairy Queen Photographer, the Handstamping Arm Licker, the Sadistic Comb Game Player, the Tea Cup Sculptor, the Traumatized Yacht Owner, the Sidewalk Psychic, the JFK Buff, etcetera, etcetera, etcetera . . .

DMITRY

Graceland

LIKE YOUR DARK GREEN BOWLING SHIRT, GRACELAND WAS ONCE SO UN-HIP THAT IT WAS HIP. SOON THEREAFTER BOTH GRACELAND AND YOUR BOWLING SHIRT WERE SO HIP THAT THEY WERE UN-HIP. THE TIDE HAS TURNED ONCE AGAIN, AND WHILE YOU SHOULD PROBABLY WAIT A FEW MONTHS BEFORE PULLING OUT THAT BOWLING SHIRT, REST ASSURED THAT IT IS ONCE AGAIN SAFE TO VISIT THE KING.
IT'S TIME TO EXPERIENCE ELVIS AS METACLICHÉ, WHICH IS DIFFERENT FROM YOUR EARLY EXPERIENCE OF ELVIS AS ELVIS, YOUR LATER EXPERIENCE OF ELVIS AS BLOATED SELF-PARODY, AND EVEN YOUR RECENT ENCOUNTER WITH ELVIS'S IMAGE STARING BACK AT YOU FROM INSIDE THAT FLOUR TORTILLA. HE IS TRULY THE POSTMODERN ICON— DEFINED BY ABSENCE, IRONY, SIMULATION, AND APPROPRIATION—AND A TRIP TO GRACELAND WILL SET YOUR PHILOSOPHICAL SLACK MIND SPINNING.

GUATEMALA

Guatemala could well be considered the slack traveler's paradise, a cheap and exotic little gem that is often overlooked by uptight bourgeois vacationers who are frightened off by tales of cholera and roaming bandits. If you see yourself as a jet-setting slacker who doesn't want to shell out the dough for a plane ticket to Tibet, Guatemala's unique cultural grab bag of beaches, jungles, drugs, and impoverished natives just might be an ideal compromise.

Your Guatemalan Experience will be enhanced by the sequence of immunizations that must be updated before your departure—polio, tetanus, typhoid—as well as the required gamma-globulin shot.

You would do well to put reports of blatant human rights abuses out of your mind while undergoing the medical preliminaries, and you should always remember to keep a sharp eye out for paramilitary activity when poking around ancient Mayan ruins.

NORTH AMERICAN PSYCHIC ENERGY HOT SPOTS

A good psychic vortex is hard to find, but for some strange reason they seem concentrated in the Southwest, which is good news for you, the wandering slacker. It's possible to make the rounds—Chaco Canyon, Cathedral Rock, Bighorn medicine wheel, Mt. Shasta, etc.—without crisscrossing the continent, and an impromptu harmonic conversion convention is often just around the next bend.

A PILGRIMAGE SCHEDULED FOR THE SUMMER SOLSTICE CAN PROVIDE YOU WITH SOME MUCH-NEEDED INSIGHT INTO THE EVER-CHANGING DEMANDS OF THE GODS. YOU PROBABLY REMEMBER THOSE HALCYON DAYS WHEN IT USED TO BE OKAY TO JUST TOSS A VIRGIN INTO THE VOLCANO AND BE DONE WITH IT. NOT ANYMORE. NOW A BUNCH OF EARTH MOTHER-TYPES WHO HAVE GOTTEN IN TOUCH WITH THE GODDESS INSIDE THEM ARE FORCED TO DRAPE THEMSELVES IN LAVENDER GAUZE AND SELL EACH OTHER HANDICRAFTS.

Keep in mind during your travels that while you're not necessarily *searching* for the doorway into the fifth dimension, if you trip over the front stoop you ought to walk on through. That, and remember that untapped electromagnetic forces can do wonders for painfully clogged bowels.

(Rule of thumb: the people who are lying in the fetal position and humming take this stuff *very* seriously. It's best not to laugh and point.)

Prague

It has been widely reported that in Prague, right now, it's Paris in the Twenties. What is it where *you* are? Berlin after World War II? Romania under Ceaucescu? Europe during the Black Death?

Prague is a bustling postcommunist metropolis that happens to be flooded with English-speaking slackers not unlike yourself. The influx of young Americans means that it is now possible to live there for months and speak nothing but English. It also means that what were once dirt cheap rents are inflating even as you read this. The city's hopping jazz bar cafe scene makes it so you can do in Prague pretty much exactly what you do right now: sit around, drink coffee, and talk.

If you fear rubbing elbows with poseurs and trust-fund slackers, Prague is probably not for you. The same goes if you're looking for the sort of "authentic" travel experience that might find you sitting on a hillside talking to a shepherd in his native language of Tosk. But where else can you go where everyone you meet will have his own "moped accident in Greece" story and be working on a loosely structured, largely autobiographical Young American Abroad novel?

Vegas

TRAIPSE THROUGH THE GULLET OF A $1 BILLION CUBIST-INSPIRED LION . . . WATCH EIGHTY TOPLESS WOMEN DANCE WHILE THE *TITANIC* SINKS ONSTAGE . . . SHORE UP A PILE OF ILL-GOTTEN GAINS . . . GET MARRIED BY AN ELVIS IMPERSONATOR . . . HEAD ACROSS TOWN FOR THE NINETY-NINE-CENT PRIME RIB . . .

IT'S TIME TO ROLL AROUND IN AMERICA'S VISCERA FOR A WHILE, AND THERE'S NO BETTER PLACE TO DO IT THAN IN A CITY THAT WAS FOUNDED BY GANGSTERS AND MADE FAMOUS BY ITS ABILITY TO ATTRACT CHUBBY OUT-OF-TOWNERS WEARING MAN-MADE SYNTHETICS. FORGET CHILDLIKE SENSE OF WONDER—VEGAS IS SCARY.

SCARY, BUT CHEAP. AND IT IS THIS VERY QUALITY—THE ABUNDANCE OF FORTY-FIVE-CENT HOT DOGS AND SEVENTY-FIVE-CENT ICE-CREAM SUNDAES—THAT WILL MAKE YOU WANT TO KEEP COMING BACK. PLAY SOME KENO, TAKE A SHOT AT THE SLOTS, PERPETRATE A LUCRATIVE SCAM, AND THEN HIGHTAIL IT TO THE I-15.

VIVA LAS VEGAS.

THE DRIVE-AWAY

Imagine for a moment someone stupid enough to hand you the keys to his automobile and let you drive it at breakneck speeds across dozens of state lines while three of your compadres entertain themselves by spilling beer on the upholstery and mooning passing station wagons. . . .

Welcome to the wonderful world of the driveaway, the slack traveler's dream come true.

A driveaway is an arrangement wherein a bloated corporate type who needs his car transported from one city to another agrees to let you—a dues-paying member of the teeming masses—drive it, simply so he can swill martinis up in business class and not waste any of his precious time motoring through Kansas. Most driveaways are coordinated by driveaway companies, which consist of a man with sweat moons under his arms whose screening process entails looking you up and down and checking your license for a convincing hologram. You can find a company in your Yellow Pages, and while each will have a slightly different policy, the following general parameters will apply:

You need:

1. A valid driver's license (not necessarily your own)
2. Enough money for gas, food, and lodging
3. A few convincing character references (employer, teacher, pothead friend posing as your pastor, etc.)
4. A flexible travel schedule

You get:

1. A functioning automobile
2. Five to nine days, and usually a limited number of miles, to deliver the automobile to its destination.

IF WHAT YOU HAVE IN MIND IS A LEISURELY TOUR OF OUR FINE CONTINENT TAKING IN ATLANTA, CHICAGO, NEW ORLEANS, AND SEATTLE, A DRIVEAWAY WON'T WORK. BUT IF YOU WANT TO BLOW FROM NEW YORK TO SAN FRANCISCO *AND* YOU'RE WILLING TO TRAVEL WITH ONLY AS MUCH LUGGAGE AS YOU CAN SQUEEZE INTO THE CAR (THE TRUNK IS USUALLY FULL), WELL, LET'S JUST SAY IT'S A *LOT* CHEAPER THAN ALAMO.
(**A WORD OF WARNING:** IT HAS BEEN SUGGESTED THAT DRIVEAWAY AUTOMOBILES ARE AN IDEAL IF NOT ALTOGETHER COMMON WAY FOR NEFARIOUS UNDERWORLD TYPES TO TRAFFIC DRUGS. BE CERTAIN TO EXAMINE THE CAR THOROUGHLY BEFORE YOU DEPART (DOOR PANELS AND ALL, JUST LIKE THE NARCS ON THE TUBE), LEST YOU BECOME SOMEONE'S PATSY AND END UP MOLDERING IN AN ARKANSAS PENITENTIARY INTO THE YEAR 2050.)

AIRHITCH

When your money is worth more than your time, you find yourself doing things like agreeing to fly into any one of several cities in Western Europe on any one of several days at virtually any time, on a flight from which you might be bumped, in order to save a couple of hundred bucks.

A couple of hundred bucks! You'd sell cross sections of your spleen for a couple of hundred bucks! Of course you'd make room for a little, shall we say, flexibility in your travel schedule in order to save that kind of cash. And that's where Airhitch comes in.

THERE ARE LOTS OF WAYS TO FLY TO EUROPE CHEAPLY—BE A COURIER, STEAL YOUR FATHER'S FREQUENT FLIER MILES, HIJACK A DOMESTIC FLIGHT AND REROUTE IT TO LUXEMBOURG—BUT AIRHITCH SEEMS TO HAVE BEEN DESIGNED WITH THE SLACK TRAVELER IN MIND. YOU REGISTER, LISTING THREE POSSIBLE DESTINATIONS IN ORDER OF PREFERENCE AND A FIVE- TO EIGHT-DAY RANGE OF POSSIBLE DEPARTURE DATES. THEY CONTACT YOU

ABOUT TWO WEEKS BEFORE YOUR TRIP, GIVING YOU A LIST OF POSSIBLE OPTIONS. YOU PICK, AND THEY TRY TO GET YOU ON THAT FLIGHT OR ONE SORT OF LIKE IT. THE ONE-WAY COST IS $169 FROM THE EAST COAST, $229 FROM THE WEST COAST, AND $269 FROM ASSORTED PLACES IN BETWEEN.

The secret of slack traveling is simple: Embrace the variables. The spirit that would have you set off for remote locales without enough money to get back home is the spirit of Airhitch. Where exactly are you going? When precisely are you leaving? Who knows? Who cares?

AT LEAST YOU'RE FINALLY GOING.

Slacker Sex

INTELLECTUAL FOREPLAY

Unfortunately, SIDLING UP TO THE NEAREST PERSON DEMONSTRATING THE CUSTOMARY CHARACTERISTICS OF THE GENDER TOWARD WHICH YOU ARE DRAWN AND SAYING, "I'M LOOKING FOR SEX AND I'LL MAKE IT WORTH YOUR WHILE" JUST DOESN'T WORK ANYMORE. SLACKERS, VIOLATING THE LAW OF THE JUNGLE AS ESTABLISHED IN JUNIOR HIGH SCHOOLS ACROSS THE NATION, HAVE DECIDED THAT BRAINS ARE A TURN-ON. IF YOUR SAT SCORES USED TO SEND MEN SCREAMING INTO THE ARMS OF THE NEAREST BATON TWIRLER, YOU WILL UNDOUBTEDLY GREET THIS AS GOOD NEWS. INTELLECTUAL FOREPLAY IS THE NEW NAME OF THE GAME.

SADLY, ONE CANNOT DEFTLY DISPLAY ONE'S PERFECTLY FORMED BRAIN THE WAY ONE CAN SHOW OFF A HARD-FOUGHT-FOR SET OF PECS. IT'S DIFFICULT TO SUBTLY PRESS ONE'S BRAIN UP AGAINST A NEW LOVE INTEREST AT A CROWDED PARTY IN A DIMLY LIT BASEMENT. NO ONE HAS DEVELOPED A SHORT SKIRT FOR THE MIND, A TIGHT PAIR OF JEANS FOR THE SOCIAL CONSCIOUSNESS, A PUSH-UP BRA FOR A COMPELLING COSMOLOGY.

AT LEAST, NO ONE HAS UNTIL NOW.

MOST OF YOU UNDOUBTEDLY KNOW ALL THERE IS TO KNOW ABOUT INTELLECTUAL FOREPLAY. IF YOU CAN DECONSTRUCT JOYCE AND RETHINK PUTEAUX CUBISM OVER A CUP OF CAMOMILE TEA AND A BOWL OF LENTIL SOUP, I ADVISE YOU TO READ NO FURTHER. MY GUIDE TO PSEUDO-INTELLECTUAL POSTURING SOLELY AS AN EXPEDIENT MEANS OF GETTIN' SOME WILL UNDOUBTEDLY TEAR AT THE FABRIC OF YOUR VERY BEING.

BUT THE REST OF YOU—THE ONES WHO WOULD LIKE TO THINK OF YOURSELVES AS RENAISSANCE PEOPLE, BUT CAN'T QUITE PUT YOUR FINGER ON WHEN THE RENAISSANCE WAS—READ AND LEARN:

RULE #1: Read reviews.

No matter how interested you are in that demure, auburn-haired cappucci-no-brewing maiden over at the cafe, you're still understandably hesitant to forego *The Simpsons* in order to read *Remembrance of Things Past*. Don't worry. *Nobody's* read *Remembrance of Things Past*.

In the interest of time, at this point you can pretty much bypass the classics. Instead, cultivate a very hip intellectualism by assiduously reading reviews and scanning the occasional brief introduction to a weighty piece of new scholarship. If you're ever asked about a particular classic, either say you read the first hundred pages in high school and couldn't get into it, or use the question as a springboard into a diatribe over canonization and the systematic marginalization of works by womyn and people of color.

RULE #2: Cultivate obscure intellectual interests.

Every intellectual has a handful of interests toward which he will steer the conversation at any given opportunity. For obvious reasons, the more arcane and tangential yours happen to be the better.

RULE #3: Get into film.

First, it's got a reasonably short, manageable history. Second, all you've got to read are the subtitles. Third, it only takes two hours to add an important work of art to your conversational arsenal. Whenever possible, steer the aesthetic debate away from art or literature and into the realm of film, and then refer to the seminal Bergman film you rented the weekend before.

RULE #4: Always tote around a thin book.

A painfully thin, well-worn book of German poetry sticking out of your coat pocket can work wonders. Likewise, a brief Kierkegaard treatise or a Samuel French play tucked in the outside pocket of your threadbare backpack. Novices often go the other direction, pretending to read *War and Peace* while sitting on their front stoop, but a thin book says infinitely more.

RULE #5: Dabble in an art.

This gives you room to spend hours expounding upon your own aesthetic philosophy, which can be as nonsensical as you well please: "My art is not Art, it is 'not-art,' meaning that while it is art, it aspires to a state of 'not-artness,' which you can tell quite clearly by this wiggly little piece of worm body dangling down from the corner of the canvas."

RULE #6: Utilize your at-home props.

While the big turn-on used to be a black lightbulb and a small jar of edible fluorescent body paint, now it's Maurice Merlean-Ponty's *Phenomenology of Perception* on the coffee table and Wittgenstein nestled next to Calvino on the nightstand. Hide anything that is incriminatingly lowbrow, not to be confused with things that are *refreshingly* lowbrow, like a weakness for comic books or a thing for *Beverly Hills 90210*.

RULE #7: Don't talk politics.

For some reason, other people's politics usually sound stupid. I don't know why, but it's true. Also, avoid religion, as other people's religions usually sound stupid, or, at the very least, seem likely to cramp your style.

RULE #8: When in doubt, keep your mouth shut.

All it takes is one "I really like Flannery O'Connor because he . . ." or a "So

you like the Pre-Raphaelites? I never could get into that medieval stuff," to blow the lid off your scam.

snob is not going to happen overnight.

Oh yeah. The Renaissance. Fourteenth to seventeenth

BUT WHO SPRINGS FOR THE CONDOMS?

The New Sex Etiquette

If you haven't figured out how to get your grubby hands on free condoms by this point in the book you are a sad excuse for a slacker. Condoms are an inalienable right in this country. NO ONE *EVER* BUYS THE CONDOMS! YOU EACH HAVE A SHOEBOX FULL OF THEM! SCAMMED FROM RED-RIBBON-WEARING SAFE-SEX PROFESSIONALS!

CONDOMS ARE THE LEAST OF YOUR PROBLEMS. BUT THIS HANDY LITTLE PUT-OUT CHART SHOULD GIVE YOU AN IDEA OF WHAT SORT OF AMOROUS EXPECTATIONS WOULD BE IN LINE WITH THE FOLLOWING TYPICAL SLACKER DATES:

THE DATE:	PROBABLE OUTCOME:
Coffee, dutch	Nothing
Coffee, he pays	Nothing
Coffee, she pays	Nothing
Accidentally meet up at after-hours bar, both drunk	Score!
Springtime bike-ride/picnic	Move in together
Stay up late watching Japanese horror flicks on video, sober	Would never happen
Stay up late watching Japanese horror flicks on video, drunk	Score!
Expensive dinner out and tickets to the theater, he pays	Would never happen
Nice dinner at home, he cooks, followed by theater tickets, she pays	Declarations of true love
Club-crowd thrash concert at which entire audience drops acid	Jointly raise accidental love child
Twelve-hour backgammon marathon followed by kitchen table drinking binge	Third base, followed by "but I think of you as just a friend" talk
Meet at basement-apartment party, spend hours discussing the dehumanization of labor and deconstructing *Horton Hears a Who*	Buy Volkswagen van together and hit the road

Just as Rome wasn't built in a day, becoming a well-read, overeducated intellectual

century.
Roughly.

BILL lives in SOUTH PHILADELPHIA in a house that he shares with four other people and works at CAFE URBANISTA, a popular slacker cafe ten blocks from his house. Up until a few months ago BILL bussed tables at OH HENRY'S, but he was caught absconding with his weight in nonperishable food items and was terminated With Extreme Prejudice. He plays the bongos and the harmonica in a band called CARPET BOMB, and does a little painting on the side. BILL'S girlfriend SUE has just finished her first short story entitled "Dreamscape 12: The Winter, Descending," and she is extremely anxious to see her name in print. BILL calls his friend ANNE, who is the lead singer of CARPET BOMB and, incidentally, also the not-infrequent target of BILL'S drunken late-night AMOROUS ADVANCES. ANNE used to be a waitron with BILL at OH HENRY'S but after seven years on the floor she leapfrogged up the career ladder to the esteemed position of BARTENDER. ANNE talks with JOE, who runs the popular weekly SONNET SLAM at OH HENRY'S, and secures a position for SUE to read her story on FRIDAY NIGHT. SUE agrees to read, but is not pacified by the concept of a LOCAL SONNET SLAM and proceeds to send her story out blindly to *HARPERS, THE ANTIOCH REVIEW, THE GEORGIA REVIEW, THE ATLANTIC MONTHLY, TRI QUARTERLY,* and, of course, *THE NEW YORKER.*

BILL'S housemate TRACY, meanwhile, has lost her job selling SOCKS at the SOCK KIOSK in the MALL. TRACY asks SUE if she knows if anyone is hiring at KINKO's, which is where SUE works part-time when she's not peddling jewelry on SOUTH STREET. SUE says KINKO'S is not hiring, but she has a friend named JERRY who does CATERING and maybe he can give TRACY some work. TRACY wanted the job at KINKO'S because she's publishing a LITERARY MAGAZINE and was hoping to get FREE PHOTO-COPYING for a week or so, and then QUIT. SUE finds this out and agrees to photocopy for TRACY while on the graveyard shift at KINKO'S.

SUE reads the first issue of *THE ROOT CHAKRA,* TRACY'S new magazine, and is mildly impressed. She gives TRACY a copy of "Dreamscape #12: The Winter, Descending," which TRACY agrees to publish in the next issue—that is, if SUE will continue to provide her with FREE PHOTO-COPYING. SUE agrees, seeing as her mailbox has been

flooded with rather brusque REJECTION LETTERS from every national LITERARY MAGAZINE known to woman.

TRACY gets a job at BOOK-ENDS, and proceeds to provide SUE, BILL, and even JERRY with 40 percent discounts on every book they purchase.

After meeting BILL at the SONNET SLAM, JOE begins hanging out at CAFE URBANISTA, eventually weaseling his way into a position as MANAGER of CARPET BOMB, a job which is as thankless as it is unpaid. JOE, however, spends a lot of time hanging out with SUE while BILL is busy on stage and the two eventually

FALL IN LOVE and MOVE TO TUCSON. ANNE succumbs to BILL'S advances late one night, but then proceeds to watch in disbelief as BILL and JERRY decide to make a life together. TRACY dies in a freak job-related accident when a wall of books falls on her and pins her to the ground, crushing her to her death. Her parents sue the pants off BOOKENDS and retire to the CARIBBEAN.

Met a Guy Who Hangs Out in This Cafe Who Knew a Guy Who Worked in a Bike Shop Where This Girl Hung Out:

THE POWER OF RELATIONSHIPS

FIRST DATE: Underground club to see Vomit Hole

SECOND DATE: WAREHOUSE CLUB WHERE FIFTEEN-YEAR-OLD ON ACID JUMPS FROM ROOF

THIRD DATE: Tacos at the House of Tacos

FOURTH DATE: HOURS OF WATCHING HER NEW BAND PRACTICE, SOME CAFE SITTING AND CARD PLAYING

FIFTH DATE: Share $275 apartment and plan on going on the road

How to Pick up Art School Chicks

BEDDING AN ART SCHOOL CHICK IS OFTEN THE TONIC OF CHOICE FOR THE LIBIDINOUS SLACKER GENT WHO HAS GROWN TIRED OF BRAINY SLACKER BABES OVERRUN WITH HANG-UPS. ART SCHOOL CHICKS ARE GENERALLY YOUNG AND UNFORMED, WITH THE SORT OF MAGPIE INTELLECTS THAT WILL NOT ONLY EMBRACE THE MOST SPURIOUS OF YOUR CONSPIRACY THEORIES BUT BE OVERHEARD ESPOUSING THEM AT THE CAFE THE VERY NEXT DAY. THEY WILL DEVOUR THE BOOKS YOU RECOMMEND, RENT THE FILMS YOU TELL THEM TO SEE, AND PRETTY MUCH DO THEIR BEST TO SHAPE THEMSELVES IN YOUR OWN IMAGE. NEEDLESS TO SAY, YOU WILL FIND ALL OF THIS QUITE REFRESHING. AS AN ADDED BENEFIT, THEY CAN OFTEN BE COUNTED ON TO PAY FOR THE BEER, PARTICULARLY IF THEIR FOUR-YEAR-LONG EXPERIMENT IN BOHEMIANISM IS BEING BANKROLLED BY A CONTROLLING SUBURBAN FATHER.

STEP 1: FIND ONE. They are the girls who a) tote around large black portfolios, and b) wear babydoll dresses and clogs. They tend to roam in packs.

STEP 2: WOW HER WITH YOUR SEARING INTELLIGENCE AND/OR ARTISTIC INTEGRITY.

This can take as long or as short as you like. It can happen during a twenty-minute conversation on the stoop outside a club she's too young to get into, or be prolonged over the course of a semester in chance afternoon encounters at your cafe.

STEP 3: SPEAK IN CRYPTIC ZEN PROVERBS AS YOU ATTEMPT TO REMOVE HER CLOTHING.

A man searched for years for a great Zen Master. When he finally found him, the roshi (Zen Master) did nothing but sit down with him every day and drink a cup of tea, and then place the cup upside down on the dirt floor. THIS WENT ON FOR YEARS AND YEARS, WITH THE BEFUDDLED SEARCHER TRYING TO MAKE SENSE OF THIS TEA-DRINKING AND HIS SEARCH FOR TRUTH. Finally, one day, as the roshi looked at the Searcher over his tea, he said to him in a voice ringing with countless years of Zen mastery, "You must empty your cup."
At that point stare into her eyes and say, "Empty your cup." Works every time.

TO THE VICTOR GO THE SPOILS: BREAKING UP

Contrary to Neil Sedaka's soulful Seventies hit, breaking up is not hard to do—*if* you do it right.

Permitting a slack relationship to get to the point where an old-fashioned breakup is in order takes some doing. Most romantic liaisons can be terminated with no more muss and fuss than a silent scramble for discarded clothing under cover of night and a few weeks of diligent call screening. But if you *do* end up surrendering your free agent status only to discover that what you thought was love was really just another narcissistic self-destructive impulse, well, you're going to have to break up.

In an ideal world you'd be able to slip out of a long-term relationship as easily as you slipped into it—semi-lucid, mildly depressed, and in a mental state in which no court on earth would hold you responsible for your actions. The problem, however, is that the slack meeting of minds and exchanging of hearts often involves the borrowing of stuff and the accumulation of joint property. Shared body fluids often equals shared friends, apartments, books, CDs, beat-up automobiles, cafes, and garage bands. What you want to do is avoid Divorce Court. What you want to do is Remain Friends.

Thus, most traditional breakup methods—like, say, coming home with the name of another woman spelled out in hickeys across your abdomen—simply won't work. You need to be mature. No matter what you say, they're going to have to face up to a harsh new romantic reality: Supply remains constant at one, demand has dropped to zero, and it's a buyer's market.

So do your best to convince him that you still love him, even though you're not *in* love with him. Let her know that she's the first non-suicidal girl you ever dated. Assure him that if he cuts down on the alcohol that little problem will iron itself out, and besides, your girlfriends told you that it happens to a lot of people. And if that doesn't work, keep in mind that possession is nine-tenths of the law and then go ahead and drop them like a lunch tray in a crowded cafeteria.

Sophie's Choice, Quiz #3

Lucky Sophie. Two wonderful men are smitten with her and ready to move into the second-floor bedroom she occupies in a house she shares with five other people. Sophie realizes that this is more than just her chance for true love—the right decision will enable her to cut her monthly rent payments in half! But despite these two young men's similarities, one is the discerning slack female's obvious choice for live-in love interest. See if you can pick who won:

NAME: Brian

DESCRIPTION: 6'1", 165 lbs. Long wavy dark brown hair, soulful brown eyes. Heads, male and female alike, turn when he enters a room.

BACKGROUND: Winnetka, University of Wisconsin, University of Texas. Currently A.B.D. toward his philosophy Ph.D.

RENAISSANCE MAN CREDENTIALS: Lead singer and guitarist for popular local thrash metal band; publishes his poems and angry diatribes in his zine entitled *Mysogeny*; occasional graffiti artist.

NARCISSISTIC SELF-DESTRUCTIVE IMPULSES: Plenty.

OTHER: Recently turned vegan; Closet *Star Trek* fan; practitioner of internal martial arts.

FAVORITE MOVIE: *Reservoir Dogs*

LAST BOOK READ: From cover to cover?

DAY JOB: Bicycle courier

NAME: Edward

DESCRIPTION: 5'10", 160 lbs. Blond hair, green eyes. Sexy in a 1950s Tab Hunter sort of way.

BACKGROUND: Raised in Atlanta suburbs, B.A. University of Virginia, M.A. in English literature from Brown.

RENAISSANCE MAN CREDENTIALS: Currently hard at work on his long-awaited first novel as well as on *Mondo Eduardo*, his upcoming one-man poetry show.

YEARS HE GIVES HIMSELF BEFORE SELLING OUT: Three

OTHER: Sometimes likes to go through life pretending he's a really flat character in a bad novel.

FAVORITE MOVIE: *Dr. Strangelove*

LAST BOOK READ: *Plausible Denial* by Mark Lane

DAY JOB: Dog walker/plant care technician/part-time cultural event usher

The Choice: Sophie let Edward move in. Brian's looks were enticing (and who the heck is Tab Hunter?), but that bit about everyone's heads turning reminded her that domestic bliss and long-hair flipping, testosterone-emitting gods-of-rock don't necessarily go hand in hand. The bicycle courier bit is, frankly, a bit of a red flag. Even though it means Brian has rock-hard buns, Sophie doesn't want to end up paying all the bills, and she's heard rumors that couriers are often somewhat irresponsible. Edward's jobs, on the other hand, bespeak a certain solidness (would you let just anyone walk your dog?); besides, that "cultural event usher" bit sounds suspiciously like "lots of free tickets." Finally, Edward's Master's from Brown is infinitely better than Brian's dissertation-less attempt at a Ph.D. Sophie dated an A.B.D. before, and she knows that if she moved in with Brian, that sad pile of coffee-stained papers passing for his dissertation would sit on her bedroom desk haunting them like the Raven.

"Nevermore . . ."

Intellectual Pretension

Pretending to Read

One of the main reasons you've chosen to slack, at least ostensibly, is so that you can have ample time to read. Not only does this sound a lot better than, say, stepping off the fast track so you can nap more frequently, but it also contributes to your image as a card-carrying member of the urban intelligentsia.

Once you manage to get the first twenty pages into enough books, you'll find that reading is sort of like watching cable, only with fewer hair replacement infomercials. Piles of partially read books scattered around your futon insure that reading never has a chance to become a chore. Mental stimulation can be as consistent or as varied as you like.

AND THE NICEST THING ABOUT READING IS THAT IT IS A RELATIVELY PAINLESS WAY TO COME DANGEROUSLY CLOSE TO ACTUALLY APPEARING TO *ACCOMPLISH* SOMETHING, DEPENDING ON **A)** WHAT YOU READ, AND **B)** WHO FINDS OUT ABOUT IT. THUMBING THROUGH *THE X-MEN* ON THE TOILET WILL NOT BE VIEWED AS AN ACCOMPLISHMENT, BUT HUNKERING DOWN WITH *FINNEGANS WAKE* IN THE RIGHT CROWDED CAFE *WILL*.

BUT WHEN IT COMES RIGHT DOWN TO IT, WHO WANTS TO READ *FINNEGANS WAKE*? THEREIN, AS THEY SAY, LIES THE RUB.

You must *pretend* to read *Finnegans Wake*. Better yet, you must pretend you have *already* read *Finnegans Wake* and *The Gulag Archipelago* and *Moby-Dick*. And you should assure new acquaintances that you've read and comprehended every word Pynchon ever penned. *The Complete Plays of Aristophanes?* —"Read it again just last week." Foucault's *The Archaeology of Knowledge* (*and The Discourse on Language*)?—"My favorite of his work." *The Critique of Pure Reason, Towards a Genealogy of Morals,* and *Either/Or?* **"CINCHY."**

12 Books to Tell Other People You've Read

- ***Being and Nothingness***, Jean-Paul Sartre
- ***Being and Time***, Martin Heidegger
- ***The Bible***, assorted authors
- ***The Brothers Karamazov***, Fyodor Dostoyevsky
- ***Das Kapital***, Karl Marx
- ***Gravity's Rainbow***, Thomas Pynchon
- ***The Magic Mountain***, Thomas Mann
- ***The Order of Things***, Michel Foucault
- ***Philosophical Investigations***, Ludwig Wittgenstein
- ***The Postmodern Condition***, Jean F. Lyotard
- ***Remembrance of Things Past***, Marcel Proust
- ***Ulysses***, James Joyce

The Slack Syllabus

-**Another Roadside Attraction**, Tom Robbins
-**Buried Dreams, Inside the Mind of a Serial Killer**, Tim Cahill
-**Beyond Good and Evil**, Friedrich Nietzsche
-**A Clockwork Orange**, Anthony Burgess
-**Delta of Venus**, Anais Nin
-**Fear and Loathing in Las Vegas**, Hunter S. Thompson
-**The Fountainhead**, Ayn Rand
-**Hollywood**, Charles Bukowski
-**The Illuminatus! Trilogy**, Robert Shea and Robert Anton Wilson
-**Journey to the End of the Night**, Louis-Ferdinand Céline
-**Juliette**, Marquis de Sade
-**The Killer Inside Me**, Jim Thompson
-**Lolita**, Vladimir Nabokov
-**The Metamorphosis**, Franz Kafka
-**Miss Lonelyhearts**, Nathaniel West
-**Naked Lunch**, William S. Burroughs
-**Querelle**, Jean Genet
-**Sandman,** Niel Gaimen
-**Siddhartha**, Hermann Hesse
-**The Stranger**, Albert Camus
-**Success**, Martin Amis
-**Tropic of Cancer**, Henry Miller

THE BOOKS WE LOVE TO HATE

Bright Lights, Big City
Electric Kool-Aid Acid Test
Generation X
Less Than Zero
On the Road
The Official Slacker Handbook
Slaves of New York
Zen and the Art of Motorcycle Maintenance

USELESS CAUSES 101

It is not totally fair to characterize slackers as apolitical. They are simply not political in any sort of recognizable, quantifiable, or ultimately meaningful sense.

But that doesn't mean that you don't have a firm grasp of the problems besetting our nation, nay, even those plaguing mankind in the aggregate. You do. And one of the more futile of your pastimes is coming up with solutions to what you see as our world's most virulent ills, solutions that you know would never even make it out of a committee in Congress, seeing as the corridors of power are greased by the filthy lucre of corrupt bourgeois capitalist scum.

PROBLEM

Cars cause a lot of pollution.

SOLUTION

Gasoline strictly rationed and eventually taxed out of existence; work day dramatically shortened to accommodate swelling ranks of suburban bicycle commuters.

PROBLEM	SOLUTION
Overpopulation causes a drain on precious natural resources.	Retooling of the economy to accommodate only clay, wool, and hemp-based products; federal license required for reproduction.
Some people live in poverty.	Everyone grouped into two-hundred-person soviets geared to produce all items necessary for self-sufficiency.
People of different nations, races, and religions tend to dislike each other.	National borders erased, religion abolished, and intermarrying enforced.
Humans often overlook how cute and fuzzy animals are.	Ban on all scientific enquiry; national vegan diet strictly imposed from above; imprisoned house pets, farm and zoo animals emancipated and permitted to roam free.
Members of the underclass often feel powerless when confronted with impenetrable monolithic economic culture.	Economically motivated crime decriminalized; idle rich corralled, stripped of all assets, and placed in "economic sensitivity training camps."
Attractive women are often ogled in public.	Ban on all secondary sex characteristics; return to quaint primordial pastime of asexual reproduction.

ARGUING PHILOSOPHY TO WIN

- **-EMPLOY THREATENING HAND GESTURES**
- -MAKE THINGS UP AS YOU GO ALONG
- **-WHIP OUT THOSE LATIN TERMS AT RANDOM**
- (*IGNORATIO ELENCHI, ARGUMENTUM AD MISERICORDIAM, ARGUMENTUM AD VACULUM*, ETC.)
- -MAKE PERIODIC USE OF PRELINGUAL VERBAL DISPLAYS
- **-WASTE PRECIOUS HOURS EXAMINING EVERYBODY'S PRESUPPOSITIONS**
- -REPEATEDLY FORCE OTHERS TO "DEFINE THEIR TERMS" TO BUY TIME TO THINK
- **-CASUALLY THROW OUT FABRICATED QUOTATIONS FROM IMPORTANT BOOKS THEY WILL BE TOO ASHAMED TO ADMIT THEY HAVEN'T READ**
- -CALL INTO QUESTION THEIR MENTAL HEALTH
- **-INSULT THEIR MOTHERS**

FILM THREAT MAGAZINE'S TOP TEN SLACKER FILMS, GIVE OR TAKE

OFFICIAL DISCLAIMER: WHILE THESE ARE ALL GREAT FILMS, WE DON'T REC-OMMEND THAT YOU GO OUT AND BUY THEM ON VIDEO. INSTEAD, BORROW THEM FROM A FRIEND AND CONVENIENTLY FORGET TO RETURN THEM. AND, ALTHOUGH THIS LIST WAS DESIGNATED THE "OFFICIAL" AND "DEFINITIVE" AND "TIMELESS" SLACKER FILM ROUND-UP DURING THE TEN MINUTES THAT IT TOOK US TO THINK IT UP, IT IS SUBJECT TO CHANGE ON ANY GIVEN DAY, DEPENDING ON OUR COLLECTIVE MOOD. SO SUE US.

Rules for being considered a true slacker classic:
1. Should stand the test of time
2. Has to star cool actors (Actors not stars!)
3. Gets even better with a six-pack

And now the movies, in no particular order. They could have been put in some sort of order, but that would require effort.

REBEL WITHOUT A CAUSE — Self-explanatory.

Easy Rider — Makes slacker parents misty-eyed and gives us a glimpse into their souls. Good on an all-night triple bill with *Five Easy Pieces* and *One Flew Over the Cuckoo's Nest*.

On the Waterfront — Marlon Brando has made a career out of playing slackers (*The Wild One, Bedtime Story, The Chase, Nightcomers,* and *Last Tango in Paris*, to name just a few) and gets bonus points for slacking off screen as well. His mumbling performance in *Waterfront* set the standard for decades of "hero" slackers.

A Clockwork Orange — Stanley Kubrick only finishes a film about once every five years or so, so even if you don't like him, you've got to admire him.

Taxi Driver — This is the ultimate "violent" slacker fantasy. However, a true slacker would find a gun and shoot himself in the foot.

Over the Edge and *Rock 'n' Roll High School* — They burn down the school.

Repo Man — "There's room to move as a frycook. I could be manager in two years."

2001: A Space Odyssey — Actually a bore, but the last twenty minutes of that colored light show is hypnotic.

Apocalypse Now — The perfect substitute for actually going to war.

Pretty in Pink — A lousy film, but ideal for a slacker seduction: The babes love it. Added bonus: made by Hollywood's biggest slacker, pathological idea-recycler John Hughes.

Rumble Fish — A slacker morality tale shot in arty black and white. Stars three generations of slacker Hall of Famers: Dennis Hopper, Mickey Rourke, and Matt Dillon.

Animal House — So good it almost makes you want to go back to college.

*- Chris Gore and **Film Threat** staff*

Unshackling The Human Spirit: The Slacker as Unrecognized Genius

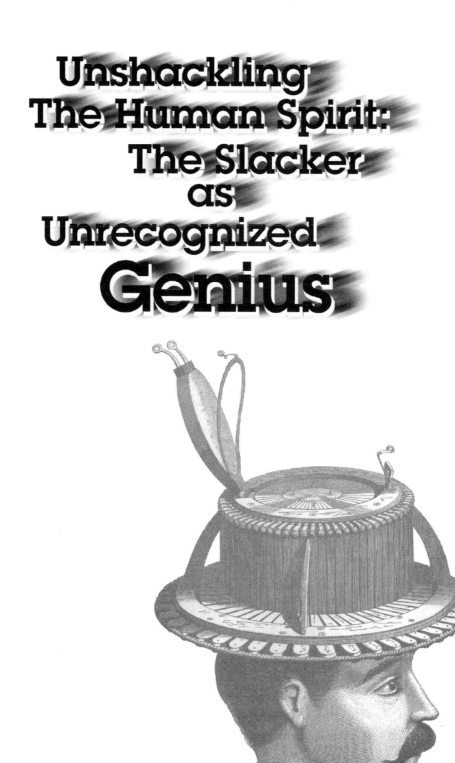

YOU AND YOUR DORMANT POTENTIAL

It's sort of like a spore.

It's a tiny hardened nugget of possibility that lies buried deep within your soul, waiting for—well, you're not sure what it's waiting for. A change of seasons? A migrating bird to swallow it and excrete it in a more suitable landscape? You to save up sixty bucks so you can buy your friend Zack's acoustic guitar? As I said, you're not quite sure. But you know it's in there. Waiting.

THE FACT THAT YOU HAVEN'T ACTUALLY *FINISHED* A SONG, OR A STORY, OR EVEN A POEM IN THE PAST SIX MONTHS DOES NOT TROUBLE YOU. YOUR THERAPIST SAYS YOU ARE UNCOMFORTABLE WITH CLOSURE. STARTING, YOU LIKE. GETTING READY TO START, YOU LIKE EVEN BETTER. LYING ON YOUR BED WITH YOUR CAT ON YOUR STOMACH, *THINKING* ABOUT GETTING READY TO START, YOU LIKE THE BEST.

IN YOUR MIND, IT IS PARIS IN THE TWENTIES AND YOU ARE ERNEST HEMINGWAY. YOUR FRIENDSHIPS (WITH EZRA, FORD, AND SCOTT, THE GUYS YOU PLAY PINOCHLE WITH AT THE CAFE EVERY DAY) ARE HALTING AND STRAINED, BECAUSE YOU REALIZE THAT YOU ARE IN HEAD-TO-HEAD COMPETITION FOR IMMORTALITY. STILL, YOU WILL BENEFIT BY YOUR ASSOCIATION WITH EACH OTHER, AND THAT THIS CRITICAL MASS OF GENIUS HAPPENED HERE AND NOW WILL BE LEFT TO FUTURE GENERATIONS TO EXPLAIN AWAY IN DOCTORAL THESES AND BLUE BOOK EXAMS.

The squalor that has come to define your existence is tolerable when you take this long-term view of your life. The fact that you don't have enough cash for cigarettes seems tragic and meaningful rather than just ever so mildly annoying. All the things you are giving up are being sacrificed in the name of Art, and if you have learned anything in the past few years it is that Art is a cruel mistress, elusive and demanding.

One day soon you will hit the mother lode. And you will look back on this time in your life with an almost inexpressible fondness, because they were the days when you toiled in obscurity rather than under the microscopic gaze of the demanding critics and your adoring public.

Busboy to luminary in a few short years.

It can, you believe, be done.

Creating a Buzz: Telling Others About Your Talent

A little local word-of-mouth fame can go a long way toward bolstering the slacker's ever-dwindling sense of self. If you can walk into a cafe and have complete strangers whispering favorably about your novel—the novel that exists as nothing more than a nubbin of an idea that rolls around in your brain, occasionally, as you are drifting off to sleep—soon the need to actually put pen to paper will subside. Then you can spend your time participating in more rewarding activities, like smoking and drinking and taking lengthy naps.

Most of the perks of being treated as a creative genius can be yours without your so much as crafting a single dirty haiku. Image, as they say, is everything, and any time or money you invest in cultivating a genius persona will be returned to you tenfold, in the form of the grudging admiration and jealousy of your peers. But forget the goatee, the heavy black glasses, the knit ski cap worn year-round, the thin brown cigarettes, the black turtleneck, the cane, the limp, the pipe, the dead grandfather's pocket watch, the shaved head, the ponytail, the dreadlocks, the beret, the bandanna-as-cap, the giant pair of jeans worn backward, the striped pajamas worn out in public—been done. What you need is something truly orig-

ALIENATION AND THE MUSE

Medium	Image	Meaning
Painting	Guy crouching in corner of windowless room	Alienation
Poetry	Guy lying on ground beneath leafless tree looking up at night sky	Alienation
Fiction	Guy committing series of bizarre, senseless, exceedingly graphic murders	Alienation

inal. Something that proclaims your disgust with the status quo as loudly as it shouts out your blinding individuality.

Once you have selected your props, you are ready to infiltrate The Scene. Remember, seeing as no living being has ever laid eyes on your creative efforts, it's up to you to be your own biggest fan. Seize every opportunity to speak favorably about your own work, while at the same time offering up insightful criticism of the aesthetic efforts of your contemporaries. Feel free to say things like "The most *powerful* short story I ever wrote centered upon . . ." or, "I felt his last short film was *tired*. Nobody wants to accuse him of running out of ideas—I mean, his early work was quite solid, in its own way—but it happens to the best of us."

It is possible to continue discreetly championing yourself for months without ever needing a second favorable opinion. Years even, so long as you don't slip up and read a poem at Open Mike Night or get drunk in public and begin excavating layers upon layers of self-doubt. When you do sense that skepticism is beginning to infect the ranks, you'll want to bring out the big guns, in the shape of evidence that you are just one small step away from "Breaking out." The easiest, of course, is to convince people that one of your scripts is "being shopped around Hollywood by an independent producer," a state that is as totally unverifiable as it is apocryphal. Having stories published in distant cities, a band making a splash on the airwaves of Berlin, demo tapes finding their way into the hands of important producers—any of these will do. The important thing is that a brand-new air of excitement is manufactured around your public persona and you continue to get the attention you deserve. When even this wears thin, and people begin pressing you in earnest to either put up or shut up, you can either resign yourself to the drudgery of actual creation or decide it's an ideal time to relocate.

The Poetry Slam

"I wrote this first poem on the bus on the way over tonight . . ."*

Welcome to the poetry slam. You are in for an evening of cutting-edge creativity and the wisdom of underappreciated urban sages. You better go get yourself a beer.

Okay, now go get another one. Which brings us to the first thing you need to know about slams, which is that they usually take place in seedy dark smoke-filled bars. Not only does the poetry seem to go down easier when there are a few shots of Jagermeister under everybody's belt, but the gritty backdrop goes a long way toward convincing everyone that the slam itself is very vibrant, very hip-very *now*. These are not poetry

weenies fed and groomed in academia. These are angry poets. These are angry *drunken* poets.

Where old-fashioned "open readings" were seen to foster mediocrity (coffeehouse poets falling prey to the flop sweats only to be greeted by polite applause, members of the lunatic fringe spouting obscenities onstage only to be greeted by polite applause, etc.), the slam was designed to reintroduce an element of objective judgment to the poetry scene proceedings. The slam was created, it would seem, so people could boo mediocrity right off the stage. . . .

". . . Last week I asked myself, 'What is poetry?' . . ."
All too often people make the mistake of going to poetry slams looking for good underground poetry. What they eventually learn is that the ideal slam is made up of the following components:

A) BITTER INFIGHTING AMONGST THE LOCAL POETS, CULMINATING IN
B) A FISTFIGHT ON STAGE.

SADLY, NOT EVERY SLAM ENDS IN A BENCH-CLEARING BRAWL. BUT EACH AND EVERY ONE HAS AT LEAST ONE POET WHO ASKS THE QUESTION "WHAT IS POETRY?" AND THEN READS A POEM THAT PROVIDES THE ANSWER. THE TRULY AMBITIOUS GO EVEN FURTHER AND ASK, "WHAT IS ART?" AND THEN READ A POEM THAT PROVIDES THE ANSWER. THIS, OF COURSE, GIVES THE IMPRESSION THAT, RATHER THAN A BUNCH OF POSTURING SEMI-TALENTS WHO WRITE POEMS ON BUSSES AND THEN READ THEM TO A DRUNKEN AUDIENCE STOCKED WITH THEIR CLOSE FRIENDS, THEY ARE INDIVIDUALS WHO HABITUALLY WRESTLE WITH IMPORTANT AESTHETIC QUESTIONS.

". . . These next few poems have, I like to believe, a very postmodern twinge. . . ."
Go to a few slams and you will realize that the only thing more fun than reading a poem in front of a large audience is *expounding* upon a poem in front of a large audience. Possible topics include:

a) What the poem is about
b) Why you wrote the poem
c) When you wrote the poem
d) Where you were when you wrote the poem
e) Who you were thinking about when you wrote the poem
f) How you wrote the poem

The opener can be as short as a dedication to Blake, or as long as a detailed description of your psychological state following your most recent drug binge. Ideally, it should function as a little window into your tortured soul, just in case your poems aren't doing the trick.

". . . And the winner of tonight's slam is (drum-roll, please) . . ."
The scoring of a poetry slam follows a very complicated point system wherein the judges, who are members of the audience selected at random, assign a point value for each poet's work. Poets score points for things including how good their poems are, whether their facial expressions are convincing, whether they shout the loudest, whether their body language looks like they practiced at home in front of a full-length mirror, whether they seem dangerously intoxicated, whether they look at the words instead of reciting them from memory, and, finally, whether or not they sometimes seem to be making things up as they go along. All of these elements are carefully rated and assigned points, which are then tabulated, just like at the Miss America Pageant, and then whoever happens to be best friends with the judges is selected as the winner.

". . . By the way, my chapbook is on sale in the back for only three bucks. . . ."

*All quotations 100 percent genuine

THE FIVE-MINUTE POET

BEGIN WITH A LOADED IMAGE YOU ENCOUNTER WHILE TAKING A WALK:
    Moth upon the asphalt, fluttering
    Wings encrusted with time, disturbing

BE PLAYFUL WITH YOUR SYNTAX:
    my daydreams, both transient and bold, unduly.

THREE WORDS: ADJECTIVES, ADJECTIVES, ADJECTIVES:
    With mock grim intensity and solemn joy,
    Your incandescent and somehow fleeting hopes scatter
    among the damaged ruins, which

REMEMBER, ALLITERATION IS YOUR FRIEND:
    Tumble headlong gasping, groaning
    into the abyss.

    Gaping.

WHEN IN DOUBT, EMPLOY THE DASH:
> If with each labored breath begins—
> a monsoon in Japan? a famine in
> Tibet?—what happens when—

WHEN TRULY IN DOUBT, RUN WITH ALL CAPS:

> SPLAT!

FOR ADDED IMPACT, STRING YOUR LINES ARTFULLY ACROSS THE PAGE:

> I silence your still small voice with the heel
> of my
> recently-reshod
> boot?

THE ART OF FICTION:
SHOWING OFF YOUR SUBURBAN CHILDHOOD SCARS

THE NICE THING ABOUT FICTION IS THAT MOST OF US LEARNED HOW TO WRITE SENTENCES IN FOURTH GRADE WHETHER WE WANTED TO OR NOT.
INDEED, WRITING IS THE ONE CREATIVE OUTLET THAT QUITE OFTEN SEEMS TO BE THE PROVINCE OF EVERYBODY. ONE SIMPLE FACT CANNOT BE AVOIDED, AND THAT IS THAT SITTING DOWN WITH A FABRIC—COVERED BLANK BOOK AND WRITING A TENDER PARAGRAPH ABOUT AUTUMN FOLIAGE IS MUCH EASIER THAN ATTEMPTING TO WRITE, PRODUCE, AND DIRECT EVEN THE LOWLIEST OF LOW—BUDGET EXPLOITATION FLICKS.
IT'S NEVER TOO LATE TO GET STARTED ON A DAZZLING CAREER AS A SHORT STORY WRITER. HERE'S HOW TO GET STARTED:

TIP #1: CULTIVATE QUIRKY WRITING HABITS

There is nothing quite so boring as a writer who wakes up in the morning and writes for a few hours and then wakes up the next morning and writes for a few more hours and then does it again each morning for years until he has completed a substantial piece of work worthy of the attention of a major publisher. The path of genius was never meant to be trod at a slow, laborious plod. Besides, if you were good at waking up in the morning and working for extended periods of time you would be a banker and drive a nicer car.

You must determine early on in your career that you need to lock yourself up in your apartment for four days, disconnect the phone and pull down the shades, strip naked, and play Dinosaur jr. over and over while you ingest performance-enhancing drugs in order to really get moving on a new short story. Not only is this infinitely cooler than the method outlined above, but the sheer number of hurdles that must be overcome (finding four back-to-back days unbesmirched by the responsibilities of gainful employment, financing the drugs, etc.) goes a long way toward explaining away your remarkably low productivity.

TIP #2: CHOOSE YOUR INFLUENCES WITH CARE

As a general rule of thumb, the more nonlinear, experimental, misunderstood, and nonsensical the better. Bukowski is the obvious choice, but any of the Beats will work. And if you happen to have a few literature courses under your belt, you might find yourself leaning toward Beckett, Joyce, Faulkner, or Pynchon, any of whom will work just fine.

TIP #3: NEVER UNDERESTIMATE THE ARTISTIC VALUE OF EXPLICIT SEX

TIP #4: YOUR OWN LIFE IS AS INTERESTING AS ANYONE ELSE'S. FEEL FREE TO WRITE ABOUT IT.

Of course you'll want to change everybody's name. And you probably ought to make your mother a blonde rather than a brunette, who grew up in Oklahoma City rather than Phoenix, and who beat you over the head with a wooden spatula rather than just annoying you occasionally with her demands that you clean up under your bed.

If you make your central character a person who lives your life, thinks your thoughts, and views the world exactly the way you do, you won't have to waste so much time making things up. That, and you can carry around a little booklet in your back pocket at all times, so you can while away the duller moments of your life scribbling sentences that can be sandwiched into your fiction at a later date: ("He thinks silently while at work, 'I'd like to come in here with a machete and hack them all to pieces.'")

TIP #5: EMPTINESS IS ALWAYS A GOOD THEME

The emptiness of popular culture. The emptiness of casual sex (explicitly presented, of course). The emptiness of life in the suburbs. Not only does this theme so accurately capture your mind-set at the moment, but it also functions as a built-in excuse for any apparent lack of depth or purpose within your story itself.

TIP #6: A BIZARRE, APPARENTLY MEANINGLESS DEATH IS OFTEN THE PERFECT ENDING FOR AN UNWIELDY PIECE OF FICTION

TIP #7: ALWAYS KEEP YOUR FICTION CLOSE TO YOUR CHEST

Your fiction will always be thought better by those who have not read it than by those who have.

This is *always* true. There are *no exceptions*.

Do not, in a fit of self-doubt, hand the first twenty pages of your novel to a close friend, seeking affirmation. You have nothing to gain and everything to lose. Your reputation as an undiscovered genius will suddenly be up for grabs, and your tirades about being a victim of a hostile literary establishment will begin to sound like excuses rather than the lamentations of a tragically misunderstood visionary.

The Slacker's Copyright

Afraid that someone might steal your work? That some envelope-opening, butt-kissing Ivy League intern at *The New Yorker* might come upon your latest loosely structured, poorly disguised piece of autobiographical fiction and try to *pass it off as her own?* Well, first get that paranoia in check, then stick a copy of your story (or poem, screenplay, comic, etching, zine, song, or photograph) in an envelope, address it to yourself, and drop it in a mailbox. When it arrives at your home, resist the impulse to open it. The date on the postmark will generally stand up in a court of law as proof that you thought of it first.

CREATIVITY: THE DARK SIDE

Match the following artists, writers, and musicians with the appropriate description of their suicides (hint: one individual listed did not take his own life):

☐ 1. Mark Rothko

☐ 2. Diane Arbus

☐ 3. Hart Crane

☐ 4. Sylvia Plath

☐ 5. Lucretius

☐ 6. Kurt Cobain

☐ 7. Ernest Hemingway

☐ 8. Virginia Woolf

☐ 9. Ezra Pound

☐ 10. Weldon Kees

☐ 11. Anne Sexton

☐ 12. Richard Brautigan

a. Jumped overboard and was drowned in the Caribbean while returning to the U.S. from Mexico.

b. Discovered lying face up in a pool of blood on the kitchen floor; apparently did an amateur job of self-sedation, then slashed arms with a razor, severing an artery at the elbow.

c. Donned mother's fur coat, poured a glass of vodka, and retired to a closed garage and started up an old red Cougar.

d. Victim of self-inflicted gunshot wound; corpse decomposed for weeks in a house in Bolinas before it was finally discovered.

e. Automobile was discovered abandoned on the northern approach to the Golden Gate Bridge; body was never found.

f. Discovered lying on side in an empty bathtub with slit wrists; body was already in a state of decomposition and journal was open to a page dated two days earlier, across which was scrawled the words "The Last Supper."

g. Although a patient and prisoner of the St. Elizabeth's Hospital for the criminally insane in Washington, D.C., for 12 years, failed to take own life.

h. Body was discovered by an electrician hired to install a security alarm; shotgun was still pointed at chin, and a suicide note written in red ink apparently ended, "I love you, I love you."

i. Brought two sleeping children glasses of milk and bread and butter, then put towels under the kitchen doors, taped up the cracks, turned on the oven, and rested head on open oven door.

j. Continued to write during periodic lucid intervals after becoming insane after taking a "love philtre." Died "by own hand" at age 44, with a famous major work uncompleted.

k. Put rocks into pockets and then walked into a river near Sussex.

l. Put on the red Emperor's robe and went into the foyer with a double barrelled Boss shotgun that had been used for years of pigeon hunting. Lowered the butt to the floor, leaned over and rested the twin barrels on forehead, and pulled the trigger.

Answers: 1b; 2f; 3a; 4i; 5j; 6h; 7l; 8k; 9g; 10e; 11c; 12d

THE "START YOUR OWN ROCK BAND" KIT

How to Name Your Band

SADLY, AS THE LINE BETWEEN IRONY AND STUPIDITY GETS PROGRESSIVELY FINER, IT BECOMES MORE AND MORE DIFFICULT TO COME UP WITH NEW BAND NAMES. EVERYTHING HAS BEEN DONE. TONGUE-IN-CHEEK RETRO POMPOSITY? FAUX-NAIF FOLKSY STRAIGHTFORWARDNESS? WHOLESALE APPROPRIATION? NAMES THAT CHANGE SLIGHTLY EACH TIME YOU PERFORM? NAMES THAT CHANGE TOTALLY EACH TIME YOU PRACTICE? COMPLEXITY? RANDOMNESS? SHEER IDIOCY? BEEN DONE.

SO RELAX. STOP THINKING THAT YOUR BRAIN CAN COME UP WITH A NAME THAT OPERATES ON ITS OWN METAPHYSICAL PLANE, A PLANE HASN'T ALREADY GIVEN RISE TO THE NAMES OF THIRTY OTHER BANDS IN TWENTY DIFFERENT CITIES. DON'T TRY SO HARD. YOU KNOW, *SLACK*:

- **Consult the back of a cereal box**
- **Flip open *Hop on Pop* and use the first two words you see**
- **Crank-call someone at 3 A.M. and employ the most creative of their expletives**
- **Ask a veterinarian for an obscure phrase of insider's lingo**
- **Drink a bottle of Nyquil and allow it to come to you in a vision**

Choosing Your Influences

BEFORE YOU GET MOVING ON THE GRITTY BUSINESS OF ACTUAL CREATION, IT'S A GOOD IDEA TO NAIL DOWN PRECISELY WHO YOUR INFLUENCES ARE GOING TO BE. NOT ONLY WILL THIS HELP YOU TO SHAPE YOUR AESTHETIC WITHOUT ACTUALLY DOING ANY WORK, BUT IT WILL ALSO GIVE YOU SOMETHING TO ARGUE ABOUT WITH THE MEMBERS OF YOUR BRAND-NEW BAND. PICK THREE FROM EACH COLUMN:

Column A	Column B	Column C
Tom Waits	R.E.M.	Nirvana
Joy Division	Led Zeppelin	The Pixies/Breeders
KISS	Pavement	Brian Eno
Volcano Suns	Galaxie 500	The Rolling Stones
Barney	MC 5	Roxy Music
Jonathan Richmond	ABBA	Schoolhouse Rock
The Stooges/Iggy Pop	Neil Young	Yo la Tengo
Elvis	Daniel Johnston	Echo and the Bunnymen
Parliament/Funkadelic	David Bowie	John Zorn
James Brown	Frank Zappa	The Doors
Ornette Coleman	Van Morrison	Jimi Hendrix
Mose Alison	Nick Cave	P. J. Harvey
Sonic Youth	Up With People	Captain Beefheart
Camper van Beethoven	Sebadoh	Elvis Costello
Big Star/Alex Chilton	Dinosaur jr.	"Free to Be You and Me"
Sly and the Family Stone	Pink Floyd	The Sex Pistols
The Fall	Cowboy Junkies	Mission of Burma
The Velvet Underground	The Velvet Underground	The Velvet Underground

Lyrical Obsessions: What's Hot, What's Not

While thinking about getting started on hammering out those lyrics, you might want to keep in mind the following trends:

Hot	Not Hot
Apathy	Suicide
Cynicism	Hope
Irony	Abject meaninglessness
Hate	Love
Alienation	Peace
Confusion	Harmony
Anxiety	Bliss
Pain	Romance
Man's inhumanity to man	Teaching the world to sing
Obsessive, ill-fated infatuation	Muskrat love

Paste Your Face Here: The Promo Shot

The Film School Dilemma

In many ways film is the ultimate slack art form. The vast number of hurdles that must be overcome, the godlike strength of will that it takes to complete even the lousiest plotless 16mm short means that failing to finish is the rule rather than the exception. Everyone knows that dozens of months and thousands of dollars stand poised like the Great Wall of China between your initial wisp of idea and the finished product, which means you can comfortably remain at the idea stage for years, decades even, without ever having to come up with anything even remotely resembling an actual movie.

Alas, this tack is not for everybody. Some of you actually want to make films. You want to be independent filmmakers, steadfastly rejecting the stranglehold of Hollywood, refusing to sell out even if your work is never seen by anybody other than your immediate family and a few close friends, all of whom, unfortunately, will say to you, "I don't get it."

You folks have two options. You can either take the autodidact route—marked by years of couch surfing, mountains of credit card debt, and the occasional moral victory in the form of cables and/or expensive equipment stolen from Kevin Costner vehicles shot on location in your town—or you can try film school.

Something about film school is decidedly un-slack. It costs a lot, quite frankly, and people try to tell you what to do. But film school can give you aspiring slack filmmakers a few things you can't find at home, even in your parents' homes: namely, access to expensive equipment, exposure at student film festivals, and introductions to powerful alums.

Choosing the right film school is as important as choosing to go at all. USC, for example, is not a slack film school. Any school that tries to make films the Hollywood way—high on bland committee consensus, low on fierce independent genius—will crush your spirit. And if, like eight out of ten slack filmmakers, you are heavily into images of rape and violence right about now, the last thing you need is a feminist critique, a Janet Reno Arm Twisting, or an unwelcome reminder of the rating system. Instead, pick a little-known school with renegade profs who are into explicit claymation epics and soundless existential art flicks, and then get to work.

If you go and discover that you were doing more meaningful work with nothing more than your father's old camcorder and special effects scavenged from your refrigerator, well, then you can be the ultimate in slack: a film school dropout.

Qualities of a Good Screenplay Writing Partner

-thinks that you're a genius
-lets you be "the concept guy"
-doesn't mind writing the entire first draft while you watch and critique
-often lets you sleep in while he gets an early jump on the work
-maintains a refrigerator stocked with free beer
-has a good sense of snacks
-is close to his father, the head of a major studio
-possesses extremely low self-esteem that ensures he will never leave you to go it alone

Alternacomix

THE UNDERGROUND COMIC WORLD HAS EXPLODED IN RECENT YEARS WITH THE HELP OF THOUSANDS OF CREATIVE INDIVIDUALS OF QUESTIONABLE MENTAL HEALTH. ONE OF THE KEY SLACK ART FORMS, THE COMIC IS AS EASY TO PRODUCE AND DISTRIBUTE AS A ZINE AND HAS EVOLVED INTO AN ART FORM WITH EXCEPTIONALLY FLUID STANDARDS OF EXCELLENCE. IT IS NO LONGER A STRICT REQUIREMENT THAT YOU CAN, SAY, DRAW IN ORDER TO BE A COMIC BOOK ARTIST. NOR IS IT IMPORTANT THAT YOU BE ABLE TO WRITE. IT IS THE CONTENT OF YOUR IDEAS THAT MATTER, AND IDEAS—PARTICULARLY IDEAS THAT THE MORE FAINT AT HEART MIGHT ASSOCIATE WITH THE PHRASE "WAR CRIMES"—ARE ONE THING THAT YOU CAN RIGHTFULLY CLAIM TO POSSESS. PERUSE A STACK OF THESE COMICS AND YOU'LL COME AWAY REFRESHED WITH IMAGES AND IMPRESSIONS LIKE THE FOLLOWING:

accidental amputations

alienated antiheroes

alien encounters

alien sex

battery acid

bestiality

bisexuality

bloodlust

bloodshot eyeballs

castration

crackhead losers

degeneracy

degradation

dismemberment

dwarfs

ether binges

evil doppelgangers

explosions

feces

grim reaper, the

gozilla

hapless antiheroes

hedonism

Should You Sell Out?

PRO	CON
You'd no longer be toiling in total obscurity.	You'd lose creative control.
You could quit your job at BookNosh and sleep as late as you wanted every day.	"Early, unrealized promise" is by far the easiest stage of any artistic career.
Your two best friends would no longer be the only people on the planet who could bear witness to your genius.	You'd soon find yourself pandering to the impoverished tastes of the masses.
You wouldn't have to fund your creative efforts with the proceeds from sidewalk sales anymore.	When faceless corporate brass hand you a pile of money to do something, they generally expect you to finish it.
You could date Kim Basinger.	Your revolutionary, neo-Marxist philosophy would have to be pablumized before they let you gab with Regis and Kathie Lee.
Everyone you went to high school with would nurse pools of envy toward you within their festering bowels.	Your parents might decide not to disown you after all.
You could afford to buy a Harley.	Your selfless vision to redistribute the world's wealth might be in jeopardy if you had 500,000 Gs in the bank.
You could hire your pathetic slacker friends to run time-consuming errands for you and give you daily back massages.	All of your lowlife acquaintances would attempt to ride on your coattails.
You'd soon be in a position to make all of your lofty goals and pie-in-the-sky projects a reality.	You'd soon be in a position to make all of your lofty goals and pie-in-the-sky projects a reality.

Are You a Temperamental Auteur or Just Another Moody Slacker?
Quiz #4

1. A local film lab refuses to develop any more copies of your film after one of the technicians catches a glimpse of the "Rape of Naples" scene. You:

    A) Wrap the processing plant in bed sheets à la Christo

    B) Photocopy your private parts and print them up on a flier with a 50 percent Off Film Processing coupon and distribute widely

    C) Use the censorship issue as a springboard for six-figure NEA grant

    D) Embark on a three-day drinking binge

2. Your newest short story, an urbane character exploration in which the bulk of the action takes place underneath the surface of the text, is summarily rejected by *The New Yorker*. You:

    A) Immediately fire off an abusive, threatening letter with a violently defaced photograph of Tina Brown

    B) Decide to reshape it into a villanelle, a French verse form marked by five tercets and one quatrain

    C) Sprinkle the f-word throughout the first paragraph and send it to a struggling local literary effort

    D) Embark on a three-day drinking binge

3. A fellow cafe-goer calls your theory that Picasso's Europhalloclasscentrism was the result of a retarded inner child, "a product of a withered little mind." You:

    A) Say, "Wither this, bud"

    B) Say solemnly, "I've met Picasso, I've worked with Picasso, and sir, you are no Picasso"

    C) Throw scalding coffee in his face

    D) Embark on a three-day drinking binge

4. You have no more money for art supplies. You:

    A) Limit yourself to media that can be shoplifted from the supermarket

    B) Hock the three piece matching luggage set you received from your grandparents at graduation

    C) Strong-arm young children in the park for their hopscotch chalk

    D) Embark on a three-day drinking binge

5. Your mother says she will buy you a new computer, but only if you agree to type up the minutes of her weekly Colonial Dames gathering. Before you even get a chance to play your first six straight hours of solitaire on said computer, she hands you twenty hand-written pages of minutes to transcribe. You:

    A) Type them up, but in the form of a Petrarchan sonnet

    B) Type them up, but add, "A motion was made to begin arming for imminent conflagration with ungrateful and sullen underclass"

    C) Sink to your knees and, in your best imitation of Brando, say, "The horror, the horror"

    D) Embark on a three-day drinking binge

6. The other four members of the garage band you started squeezed you out in a secret midnight meeting to which you were not invited, because they "no longer felt they were in need of a mouth organist." You:

    A) Steal the amps and skip town

    B) Start a rumor that the lead singer worships Phil Collins

    C) Stage a grisly quadruple murder/failed suicide and watch from a hospital bed as your next-door neighbor is interviewed on *Inside Edition*

    D) Embark on a three-day drinking binge

Scoring: For each A, B, or C you chose, give yourself 0 points. For each D you chose, give yourself 1 point. A perfect score of 5 earns you Temperamental Auteur status. Anything less than that means you're just another Moody Slacker.

Inside The **Twisted** Slacker Psyche

MARTIANS VS. MASONS:
CHOOSING A CONSPIRACY THEORY

When choosing a conspiracy theory to investigate, you should start out with an unsatisfactorily explained national tragedy—like the Jonestown massacre or the crash of Pan Am Flight 103—or an ominous indication that things are not altogether what they seem: the News Election Service's chokehold on our election process, say, or the Council on Foreign Relations's all-pervasive influence over our foreign policy.

Let's say you decide to begin with an open-ended hypothesis along the lines of: "Jim Jones: bush-league anti-Christ or hypnoprogrammed genocidal racist on the CIA payroll?" Start poking around. Ask some questions. Skim a few tracts you steal from the anarchist bookstore. Talk for four hours with a cafe-dweller who thinks that the bump on his nose is evidence of a monitoring device implanted deep inside his right nostril by a sadistic extraterrestrial biologist. Read a dog-eared, out-of-print paperback whose preposterous theories outlined on page one don't seem quite so preposterous

by page 297. Lie in bed. Stare at the inside of your eyelids. *Think.*

Slowly, you'll start putting the pieces together. You'll realize that something smells fishy, more fishy than you would expect if you were simply dealing with run-of-the-mill incompetence, avarice, terrorism, insanity, satanism, or illegal CIA activity. A cartoon light bulb will appear over your head: There Is Order to All This Evil. There is, you realize, a Pattern.

Once you settle on the notion that all forms of evil are fundamentally interconnected, you are in a position to determine culpability. You are in a position to seek an answer to The Question.

It is of course impossible to do justice to the science of UFOlogy in a limited forum such as this. There are as many theories as there are theoreticians, maybe even more. Perhaps the only thing resembling a general consensus is that the gov-

ernment is not revealing everything it knows. Project Blue Book and Project Grudge are universally regarded as official snow jobs. But the fact that the Air Force has in its possession nine extraterrestrial craft which it studies at the top secret Nellis Air Range in Central Nevada, or that four different races of aliens have ben captured and monitored by our higher-ups, or that leaders in Washington and Moscow are, in fact, in cahoots with our secret alien overlords is, frankly, mere speculation.

While UFOlogists of all stripes take the governmental cover-up for granted, many intriguing questions remain to be debated. Are the aliens visiting our planet benevolent, albeit misunderstood, real-life ETs? Or are they sadistic and cruel, intent on using earthlings as a source of amusement, labor, sexual gratification, and—heaven forbid—food? Did they first arrive sometime after 1945, intrigued by the detonation of the atomic bomb at Alamogordo, New Mexico, or have they been visiting for hundreds of thousands of years and

ALiEN LEXiCON

ACONIN: A(nother) CON(scious) IN(telligence)

BEFAP: BE(ing) F(rom) A(nother) P(lanet)

ETI: E(xtra) T(errestrial) I(ntelligence)

GALAXIAN: Generic term applying to all beings from a particular galaxy

MANADIM: MAN(ifestation from) A(nother) DIM(ension)

NEBECISM: The theory that advanced beings from elsewhere in the universe influenced man's evolution and history

OPTIMAN: OPTI(mum) MAN, an earthling who has been modified to endure the stress and tension of an interstellar journey

UFONAUT: Intelligent being who pilots a UFO

USO: Unidentified Submarine Object

ZEROID: Creatures or animals that live in space

deliberately accelerating the evolution of man? Do they make use of black holes or similar "space gates" to travel enormous distances through the universe, or do they come from a space-time continuum that is parallel to our own? Are they trying to keep us from hastening our own extinction, or do they

purposefully sow worldwide strife to keep us from joining arms and waging war with them? The pendulum swings of speculation stem from conflicting reports of various UFO contactees. Classic alien sex/kidnapping contactee cases like that of Antonio Villas-Boas of Brazil indicate that perhaps the aliens simply hope to introduce half-human love children to their native planets. Others attribute the "missing person" phenomenon to whole scale alien abduction, reporting that, while they were allowed to leave the spaceships after a period of time, countless humans remained trapped inside. Finally, if the aliens *are* calling the shots in an intergalactic conspiracy of unfathomable dimensions, you can rest assured that there would be a massive disinformation/propaganda machine set in place, and people who tried to speak out would be publicly ridiculed and placed on the cover of *The Weekly World News* right along side Monkey Boy and the Woman Who Has No Head.

MASONS

Just as employing the vernacular "Martians" doesn't mean that you believe that

our space visitors hail from Mars, casually using the word "Masons" to refer to secret societies involved in conspiracy doesn't necessarily mean that you think your uncle Wayne, a Masonic initiate, is on a quest for total domination of the world. Indeed, state-of-the-art conspiracy theory pretty much leaves the Masons alone, except insofar as they serve as a recruiting camp for the real bad guys, the true conspirators: The Illuminati. The Illuminati—or the Ancient Illuminated Seers of Bavaria-are on a quest for total domination of the world. They are the personification of Nietzsche's will to power. Their nefarious goal is to bring about one world, ruled by a top secret cabal of five Illuminati elites, in which personal liberty and freedom as we now know it will cease to exist. Now, briefly: The Illuminati were started (or revived, depending on whom you listen to) on May 1, 1776, by Adam Weishaupt, a defrocked Jesuit and thirty-second-degree Mason residing in Bavaria. He subsequently traveled to America, killed George Washington, and served as our nation's first president for two terms (which explains both the infamous pot crop at Mount Vernon and why portraits of Washington look like they were modeled on two different men). Weishaupt's thinking resulted from the collision of German mysticism with the Enlightenment, and his theories eventually incorporated both an Outer Doctrine and an Inner Doctrine, the latter of which likeness on the front. Everything from the first four notes of Beethoven's Fifth Symphony (da-da-da-DUM, morse code for V, Roman numeral meaning 5, a sacred number for the Illuminati) to the first line so their strategy is obfuscation.

Illuminati theory explains the strangely inevitable quality of America's drift toward totalitarianism and why party politics so often seem like nothing more than a massive confidence trick. And the push for gun control laws, the concept of computerized fingerprinting to prevent entitlement fraud, law enforcement's abuse of electronic surveillance, and the much-hyped "war on crime" all take on a slightly ominous tone when you think that invisible forces behind our government are trying to saddle us with a worldwide dictatorship that will last forever.

novus ordo seclorum:
MASONS IN THE WHITE HOUSE

Ronald Reagan
Gerald Ford
Harry Truman
Franklin Delano Roosevelt
Warren Harding
William Taft
Teddy Roosevelt
James Garfield
Andrew Johnson
James Buchanan
James Polk
Andrew Jackson
James Monroe
George Washington

Plus just about every last signer of the Declaration of Independence (including Benjamin Franklin).

articulated a conspiracy to rule the world.

The Illuminati don't really care if you know they exist. They put their pyramid with the eye on the back of the dollar bill and their leader's of *Moby-Dick* (where Melville tells you he's a disciple of Hassan i Sabbah) tells you that the Illuminati are real. They are smart enough to realize that they can't remain completely hidden,

Conspiracy a-go-go

The JFK debacle was just the tip of the iceberg, the papery skin of an onion that you could peel for a lifetime—from Oswald to the Commies to the Mafia to the Cubans to Castro to the CIA to George Herbert Walker Bush—without ever uncovering the real truth, the True Conspiracy.

Most Americans are content to sit back in their straddle-loungers and swallow the self-serving propaganda served up by the ruling elite. But not you. Your ears perk up when you hear the words "Trilateral Commission." You anxiously scan the classified ads searching for thank-yous addressed to St. Jude. You break into a cold sweat when you stumble upon the word "fnord" printed in *The New York Times*.

Test your conspiracy theory know-how by taking the following quiz:

True or False: In 1888, Cecil Rhodes created a secret society to establish total domination of the world by the English, which continues to function to this day through Oxford University, Rhodes Scholarships, and the Council on Foreign Relations, and is underwritten by Morgan and Rothschild banking interests.

True or False: Adam Weishaupt, founder of the Order of Illuminati, killed George Washington and served himself as our first president for two terms. The Illuminati are ultimately responsible for the French Revolution, the Bolshevik revolution, the American Revolution, the Pope, the Kennedy assassination, the Manson family, the Rockefeller dynasty, the numbers 5, 17, and 23, the New Age movement, The Nazis, UFO visitations, the Universal Price Code, and the pyramid with the eye on the back of the dollar bill.

True or False: The Gulf War never actually took place.

True or False: Abbie Hoffman—Sixties wild-eyed pot-head radical, Eighties entrenched well-paid radical—was actually a CIA *agent-provocateur*.

True or False: The Jonestown massacre was actually part of a mass mind-control experiment by the CIA, a renegade offshoot of the top-secret MKULTRA program, which experimented with hypnotism and LSD in an effort to create a guilt-free, mind-controlled Manchurian Candidate assassination.

True or False: Posing as a petrified hippie rock band, The Grateful Dead is actually a British Intelligence operation in deep cover.

True or False: Human beings are a slave race living and breeding on an isolated planet in a minor galaxy. Once a prime source of labor for our extraterrestrial slave lords, we remain to this day their possession. Our planet's wars and disasters are part of their effort to control us and keep us imprisoned, and the plague that killed one-fourth of the population of thirteenth- and fourteenth-century Europe was actually an act of biological warfare by our alien custodians.

True or False: David Rockefeller's Trilateral Commission, the Council on Foreign Relations, and CIA-front Exxon are the visible outcroppings of a shadow government intent on immanentizing the Eschaton so a powerful few can seize complete control of the world.

True or False: Sirhan Bishara Sirhan, who confessed to killing Robert F. Kennedy, was actually an unwitting patsy hypnoprogrammed by the CIA. The LAPD—infiltrated by CIA operatives—overlooked the impossible angle of the fatal shot, the extra bullets found in the pantry, and the "woman in the polka-dot dress" during its haphazard investigation of the assassination.

True or False: *Newsweek* is a CIA publication.

True or False: As Kissinger protégé, CIA agent, Skull and Bonesman, Trilateralist, Bildeburger, Council on Foreign Relations member, Texas oil man, and cheerleader for a New World Order, George Herbert Walker Bush is a cryptotalitarian and the point man for a cabal of elites who are tireless in their quest for total world domination.

Bonus:

True or False: Bill Clinton—Rhodes Scholar, Member of the Council on Foreign Relations, Trilateralist, and Bildeburger—was spawned in a netherworld where "left" and "right," and "liberal" and "conservative," no longer have any meaning, and was placed in power by precisely the same shadow government that put George Bush into power.

Answers:

If I reveal the truth, I will in all likelihood be chopped into pieces, wedged into an oil drum, and left bobbing for all eternity in an isolated inlet off the Arctic Ocean. Hence, I will demur.

IS THAT A SAFETY PIN IN YOUR NIPPLE OR ARE YOU JUST GLAD TO SEE ME?: SLACKING THROUGH RITUALIZED PAIN

The slack existence is tailored to both numbing life's pain and plumbing its depths. In so far as anything smacking of fatalism catches the slacker's eye, those halfhearted dabblings in ritualized pain ought not shock. What could be better than excruciating torture capped with a postprocedure endorphin high?

Still, scrotal piercing is not for everyone. Slackers might live where the subcultures collide, but urban primitives you are not. And the fact that you would sooner remain in bed for a week than jog around the block suggests that, deep down, you are somewhat pain-averse.

But tattoos fulfill your longing for permanence in a landscape dominated by dead shopping malls and flimsy tract houses. And—even though preteens in Idaho caught on about six months ago—piercing still seems seductively transgressive. You've seen one too many musicians set themselves on fire onstage to remain immune to the artistic appeal of self-mutilation. Slam the door on normalcy. Deface yourself.

(Alas, elaborate Celtic tattoos, bull rings, and erogenous-zone piercings are fast becoming yesterday's news. Brace yourself for the waves of the future: abstract expressionistic body inking, branding, and ritualized amputation.)

THE PARANOIA CHECKLIST

☐ I refuse to send any of my screenplays out to Hollywood because if I do somebody will probably steal my ideas.

☐ I conduct all of my personal financial transactions in cash or money order to restrict the amount of personal information about me circulating in national data bases.

☐ Sometimes I worry that my telephone might be tapped.

☐ I believe that the FBI maintains a file on me.

☐ I know too much about The Conspiracy for my own good.

☐ The light fixtures at the cafe where I hang out each day are probably bugged.

☐ I'm afraid that there is a high-tech tracking device of some sort imbedded in one of my molars.

☐ I have seriously considered staging my own death and assuming an alternate identity in order to thwart those who want to do me harm.

☐ Sometimes I feel like I'm probably a product of a Nazi breeding experiment.

☐ I think the aliens who visit my bedroom late at night want to have sex with me.

THE INNER PAIN CHART:
WHAT YOUR TATTOOS SAY ABOUT YOU

Tattoo	Meaning
Tasmanian Devil on your inner thigh	Sublimated Oedipal aggression

Tattoo
Skull and crossbones in pool of blood on the nape of your neck

Meaning
Defective superego

Tattoo
"Bad Seed" printed in Chaucerian font on your deltoid

Meaning
Entrenched defensive ego

Tattoo
Satan's like-
ness on
your
abdomen

Meaning
By-product
of a drink-
ing binge

Tattoo
Snake on
your arm

Meaning
Anxiety
about your
penis

Tattoo
Ancient Celtic
cross on your
breast

Meaning
Fear of intimacy

Tattoo
Butterfly on
your butt

Meaning
Unresolved
Cinderella
complex

Tattoo
Barbed wire
encircling your
ankle

Meaning
Thwarted God
complex

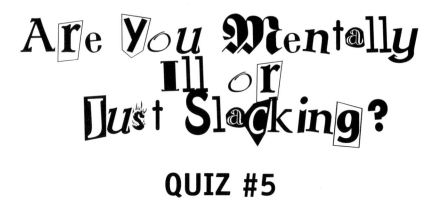

QUIZ #5

Choose the answer that best matches your own:

1. The dark brown water stain slowly growing on the ceiling over my bed:
   a) Spooks me sometimes late at night
   b) Probably is causing the asbestos to flake down onto my Scooby sheets
   c) Reminds me of a powerful story by Flannery O'Connor
   d) Resembles a handsome young Ronald Reagan

2. If I could have any single superpower, I would pick:
   a) The ability to turn my limbs into ropes on a moment's notice
   b) The "Form of . . . an Ice Helicopter" half of the SuperTwin powers
   c) The capacity to send a threatening tidal wave back out to sea with a single breath
   d) The power to transmute everything within the entire known universe into antimatter by touching my right index finger to my nose

3. The voices in my head sound strikingly similar to those of:
   a. Ginger and Mary Ann
   b. Vera and Flo
   c. Leather and Pinky Tuscadero
   d. Margaret Thatcher and Cokie Roberts

4. Sometimes when I'm lying alone on my futon all day I like to imagine:
   a) I'm adrift on an ice floe in the north Atlantic, and unless someone rescues me I'll have to slaughter one of these cute baby seal pillows in order to survive
   b) I'm the last human on the planet earth, and if I so much as open my bedroom door I'll be struck down by a mysterious Andromeda virus and meet a lingering, painful death
   c) I've been abducted by creatures from a parallel dimension, and now I'm being forced to lie motionless on this gravity pad until they return to perform more experiments of a sexual nature on me
   d) What it would feel like to kill someone with my bare hands

5. The *Hard Copy* regular I most strongly identify with is:
   a) Princess Fergie
   b) John F. Kennedy, Jr.
   c) Tatum O'Neal
   d) The disgruntled postal worker

6. My favorite book as an adolescent was:
   a) *Are You There God, It's Me Margaret,* because it dealt frankly with
      girls getting their periods
   b) *Then Again, Maybe I Won't,* because it dealt frankly with erections
      and wet dreams
   c) *Forever,* because it dealt frankly with young people losing their virginity
   d) *Alive,* because it dealt frankly with the eating of human flesh

7. My life would be much better if only I had:
   a) Movie-star good looks
   b) A bankable screenplay in preproduction
   c) Enough quarters to do my laundry
   d) A few fewer personalities

SCORING: Give yourself 1 point for each A, B, or C, and 2 points for each D.

7 points:	Tell your parents to stop worrying. You're just slacking.
8-9 points:	Candidate for Prozac.
10-13 points:	Candidate for Lithium.
14 points:	Candidate for shock treatment at the Shady Tree Hospital for the criminally insane.

YOUR SLACKING DAYS ARE OVER WHEN YOU . . .

WITHDRAWN

-Linger in front of J. Crew

-Join a gym

-Feel vague anxiety when examining your tattoos

-Begin attending church regularly

-Apply The Patch

-Buy *What Color Is My Parachute?*

-Are institutionalized

-Order Sanka

Appendix

Daily Affirmations for the Slacker

My "Self"   **Monday**
I have consciously elected to avoid any meaningful participation in society. Instead, I choose to participate meaningfully within the bounds of my Self. The nice thing about this is that I can do it in bed. If I want. Or I can do it while watching reruns of *Small Wonder*. It doesn't matter. It's up to me. Me, and my Self.

Taking Control   **Tuesday**
I will not live a life defined by arbitrary "shoulds" and "musts" imposed upon me by others. When my boss says to me, "You'd better do such and such or I'll fire your lazy ass," I will respond with a self-affirming statement like "Oh yeah, bud? I'll slap a discriminatory firing suit on you so fast you'll think you're being stalked by the ACLU."

I Am an Individual   **Wednesday**
I will not be categorized. I refuse to align myself with a political party, because doing so would only place more power into the hands of the Ruling Elite. Of course, I prefer to have liberal Democrats in office because the Republicans aren't going to help me with things like welfare fraud. But beyond that, I really don't care.

Setting Boundaries   **Thursday**
I am free to set my own boundaries. I don't have to subject myself to abusive correspondence from individuals attempting to extort financial payments from me. I don't have to answer their telephone calls, either. I have studied up on ways to stage my own death and assume an alternate identity in order to get out of paying back my student loans. If they push me hard enough, I just might do it.

Remuneration   **Friday**
A paycheck is not a report card on life. Indeed, I have found that it usually works to my advantage to be paid under the table. Being paid in cash substantially reduces the amount of money I am legally responsible for handing over to the IRS. Fortunately for me, the IRS does not even know I exist.

Squandered Potential   **Saturday**
Extrinsic rewards do not interest me. I can choose to pursue a life of inner evolution rather than one of material gain. When my parents tell me that I am squandering my potential, I am strong enough to tell them that the only thing I have not been squandering is my potential. I am secure in the belief that my potential remains unsquandered.

Sanity   **Sunday**
You cannot put a price on sanity. Unfortunately, my nonexistent health insurance package does not cover the costly Jungian analysis for which my present state would suggest I am an ideal candidate. Thus, on this holy day I choose to be ministered to by the Great Comforter. I am content, as always, to remain horizontally integrated into life.

About the Author

Sarah Dunn
graduated from the
University of Pennsylvania in 1991,
and is currently at work on her next book.